How To Get Your Kid

OFF DRUGS

Scott Wisenbaker

Wisenbaker Media

DENTON, TEXAS

Scott Wisenbaker/Wisenbaker Media
PO Box 448
Denton, Texas 76202
www.scottwisenbaker.com

How To Get Your Kid Off Drugs/Scott Wisenbaker. – 1st ed.
ISBN-10: 0-9980869-0-8
ISBN-13: 978-0-9980869-0-3

Cover by Mark Lewis

Acknowledgments

Writing this book has been an eye-opening experience that demanded clarity of thought, patience, and perseverance. This book was subjected to three very different edits. I would like to thank Rachael Goldstein, from Philadelphia, PA for her initial rough draft edit. I would like to thank Leslie Wisenbaker and Jan Pompei who edited the book for content and factual accuracy. Lastly, I would like to thank Lana Wisenbaker who completed a final edit for flow and readability. It has been our goal to make this book as easy to digest as it is to comprehend for the family member in need.

Special Thanks

To the many who directly or indirectly inspired and aided throughout the process of writing this book.

First and foremost, I must recognize and thank my team and family at Solutions of North Texas. I would also like to thank Brent Snyder; Myers Raymer; the Honorable Steve Burgess, Texas 158th Judicial District Judge; the Honorable Doug Robison, Texas 393rd Judicial District Judge; the Honorable Coby Waddill, Judge, Denton County Criminal Court No.5; Ken Metcalf, Director, Denton County Juvenile Probation; the Denton Police Department; the Denton County Sheriff's Department; Captain Jeff Davis DCSO; Lori Vann, MA, LPCS; Kevin Edwards; Ron Chase; and all of my friends and colleagues in the addiction treatment, recovery, church, and legal communities.

Lastly, I would like to thank the Coffee and Cigar Group. I value the time we all have together.

Forward

Over 10 years ago, well over, I first heard Scott speak at a monthly gathering of defense attorneys. I wish I could say he was spellbinding and riveting, but he wasn't. Instead, what he had to say was absolutely so! He had reached out to us to give us what many of our most desperate clients needed: hope. At the time, Scott had just opened his first house, near a local university, that provided drug addiction treatment in a residential setting. What was miraculous, initially, was the cost! Hope, for less than what a minimum wage job pays monthly. He still adheres to that standard.

I had always represented folks with limited resources. That means many couldn't afford to pay me my full fees, much less 20 times that on monthly fees at a facility for the rich and famous. That leaves a HUGE number of desperately addicted people without an effective alternative. Scott provided that alternative. I believe one of the first clients I sent to him had a raging poly-substance addiction that included heroin, alprazolam (Xanax), and other substances. That person ended up staying for at least six months at his facility/home. That client was the first in a long line of my clients who came back to let me know how successful they were in the program. I have had clients who had pending Child and Protective Services cases in conjunction with their pending drug cases who were able to earn the right to have their children returned to them. Many started the journey with little self-respect left, no skills to speak of, and haunting problems from their youth. Scott and his staff started with building their self-respect and demonstrating to them their value. His program has given many of my ex-clients the skills to survive the daily stresses that most folks are able to move past. He has helped my people regain and earn their self-respect. Many who have had their childhoods stolen have learned to live with those ghosts and put them in the past, through his help.

It was only after I took the bench that I discovered that Scott had gone through the Dallas Court System over 20 years ago with Judge Creuzot, the District Judge who started the Dallas Drug Divert Program. Judge Creuzot refused to allow Scott to quit. This means he put Scott in jail whenever Scott had issues or wouldn't take responsibility for his actions. He never gave up on Scott, something Scott has carried over to his program. Scott forces people in his program to take responsibility for themselves. His staff comes from the ranks of those who have been successful in the program. They aren't willing to accept excuses. They have all been through their own addiction issues.

Where Scott leads and shines is where most fail. He communicates. He brings together the stakeholders in the community. He began by reaching out to the churches and the police, understanding that they are at the front lines of addiction. I'm sure from his experiences he recognizes that the police are doing what they can to rescue folks with addiction. The church is where the desperate often turn first. He reached out to attorneys. He spoke with county law enforcement and was able to get an agreement to allow his staff into the jail to evaluate those who requested his services. He has founded multiple monthly gatherings of service providers (medical, social, housing, addiction, counseling, etc.), where each can relate what they are doing. For years, Scott has spoken and led panel discussions at state and nationwide educational and industry gatherings. He has asked probation officers, attorneys, and judges to speak with him, to educate the industry on the interrelationship of the courts, probation departments, and counseling providers, so that there is mutual respect and understanding. He understands that everyone is working toward the same goal.

I tell people that Scott has been through addiction, understands addiction, and has helped others move past addiction. Because of the interrelationship between mental health and addiction, Scott understands and has helped treat those people who have such issues. He currently provides a staff member from his facility, who works with the Denton County Mental Health Court. He is assisting with the development of the Denton County Drug Treatment Court, which includes programs for educating first-time offenders and treating those with larger addiction issues.

Steve Burgess
Texas 158th Judicial District Judge

INTRODUCTION

I wrote this book for those family members or close friends of an addict who are consumed with trying to keep their loved one alive. I will tell you exactly what to do and how to do it.

My name is Scott Wisenbaker and I have been clean and sober since March 20, 1995. For years, I struggled with addictions that included alcohol, marijuana, cocaine, and methamphetamines. As a result, I was arrested many times from 1982 to 1995. In 1995, I sat in the Dallas County Court holding tank for the very last time. After years of losing everything I held dear, I was finally brought to my knees inside the jail just a month earlier when I realized I would never be free if I continued in my addiction.

So why would you listen to anything I have to say?

I understand the mind of an addict and have successfully helped thousands take control of their addiction and return to being productive members of their families and society. I will tell you the very same thing I have told thousands of men and women in jail. I am the guy who knows how to get off drugs and stay out of jail. They are not interested in what trainings I have attended or what I do for a living. They simply want to know how I did it. The idea being that if someone like me could do it, maybe they could as well. I remember the very first time I ever made that simple statement that I continue to use to this day. Sitting in a room surrounded by offenders who wanted to know who I was and why they should listen to me, it just came out: "I am the guy who knows how to get off drugs and stay out of jail." The room became quiet and I started to tell them about where I had been and how I was able to beat my addiction.

A decade later, I took my mission a step further and opened my first long-term residential facility in 2006. I would show those who suffered with addiction how to overcome their disease, return to the workforce, become self-sufficient, repair their past, and find purpose in life. Since the inception of my program, we have made contact with, advised, or consulted with nearly 8,000 people. That represents nearly 8,000 families. We have made contact with countless men and women in Texas jails. Over 1,500 men and women have entered into our long- term residential program.

I personally have helped develop and currently serve on two specialty drug courts while a member of my staff serves on two other specialty courts in Denton County. I remain in the constant pursuit of knowledge and training in leadership, treatment, crisis intervention, court procedures, and law enforcement. My work and relationships within the legal community have afforded me the unique opportunity to take part in training law enforcement as well as receive training that has to this point been reserved for law enforcement personnel.

I simply believe that the more I learn and the more I teach, the more suited I am to continue my mission.

It is important (and maybe even critical) that you read the entire book. It contains pertinent information that will help you understand the realities of addiction, symptoms to look for, treatment options, how to work with the legal system and, most importantly, options for dealing with the addict you love so dearly.

CONTENTS

CHAPTER ONE

MYTHS AND TRUTHS ABOUT ADDICTION

It was odd that the guard shack was empty but the gate was wide open.

Rounding the corner, Dave could see the reflection of what seemed a thousand red and blue flashing lights. "Is that my house?" he asked himself. His pulse started beating in his chest and he broke out in a cold sweat. He didn't even remember parking his car.

Racing towards his house, there was a burning in the pit of Dave's stomach just as his wife started crying uncontrollably. In what seemed to be the longest run of Dave's life, he shoved at least three first responders out of his way. Just short of the front door, Joe stopped Dave in his tracks and wrapped his arms around him, moving Dave back.

"You have to stop!" Joe cried.

With tears running down his face Dave replied, "Uniform or not, if you don't let go of me I am going to run right through you!"

Holding Dave even tighter, Joe then said something that will haunt Dave for the rest of his life. "It's Steve . . . I'm so sorry but he's gone, Dave, but we have to complete our investigation."

Joe later explained that Dave's 17-year-old son had aspirated and died from a suspected heroin overdose. Heroin?

As Joe was talking, the sound of his voice faded. In fact, every sound faded. All Dave could hear were the shrill cries coming from his wife. He could feel anger and depression fighting for control of his mind, but he could hear only his wife and see only flashing lights.

In an instant, Dave's dreams left and he became numb to the world.

So let's get right to it.

You are afraid that your child or someone else close to you is going to die. Is that not why you picked up this book amidst the tens of thousands of self-help books, guides, and videos?

You are already waiting for that dreaded phone call or the appearance of the police at your door. I want to help you deal with that fear.

There are two things I want to convey right from the start:

1. I know and understand your fears. I walked through the most difficult time of my life, and I emerged with an overwhelming desire to help others stave off these painful and unnecessary tragedies. I have buried more people I love than I care to think about. I know how to help prevent such outcomes.

2. This book is very direct and to the point. I have been told that I have little tact in these matters, but I believe there is no time for tact or subtlety. I will be speaking to you as an alcoholic, a parent, and a treatment provider; to the very best of my ability, I commit to speak both truth and hope to you.

The first truth everyone needs to understand is that when someone is using drugs like opiates, pain pills, or heroin, the mortality rate is very high. These drugs are incredibly dangerous. That isn't hype; it's fact. These drugs can quite possibly kill someone the *very* next time they use them, so, again, there is no room for tact. What you need to understand is that by taking action, you will reduce the chances of tragedy; however, if you do nothing and allow your loved one to continue down the same path, the odds that you will realize your greatest fear greatly increase.

Throughout the course of this book, I will teach you how to immediately decrease the odds of tragedy and greatly increase the odds of a favorable outcome. Part of that process involves taking an honest look at what is going on with drug use in our culture.

THE WHY OF ADDICTION

So why would people ever put themselves in such a dangerous situation? Why wouldn't they avoid drugs and alcohol if they know they could lose everything and everyone who is precious to them? Why would anyone ever start a habit he knows will eventually kill him? For instance, why would anyone ever start smoking cigarettes after that was proven to be deadly? These are great questions. There are many different answers and theories, but the reality is that we often make bad decisions and consume things that we know are bad for us.

We start using drugs and alcohol because we like the way it makes us feel. Sometimes we are trying to fit in or forget something troubling to us, but the very first time we used we were excited. We wanted to know what it felt like to be drunk or high. The sense of ease and comfort we found guaranteed that we would do it again. We were doing something naughty and it felt really good. Suddenly, we understood certain jokes in movies. We may have felt we had discovered something new and wonderful. We could not comprehend that something that felt so good could actually be bad for us, despite what we had been told. It was our secret and for the first time we felt as though we had found something that was truly ours.

The American culture in great measure is built around alcohol. We love it and we can't get enough of it. Weddings, sporting events, business deals, dating rituals, holidays, and accomplishments, large or small, are openly celebrated with alcohol.

When was the last time you attended a wedding with no alcohol? I have been clean and sober since 1995 and I can count on one hand the weddings that I have attended where alcohol wasn't involved. Even when the couple getting married does not drink, there always seems to be libations for others. It may only be the champagne toast, but it's there. We learn from a young age that alcohol is for celebrations.

And what about sporting events? The end of the World Series, Super Bowl, Stanley Cup, NBA Playoffs, and NASCAR all involve celebrating with large bottles of champagne; that is how we see others celebrate. They may dump Gatorade over their coach's head on the football field, but it's champagne they're drinking in the locker room.

What about television commercials? How many beer commercials do you think are broadcast during the course of just one football game? What about the commercials for liquor or prescription drugs that promise to make us feel better, sleep better, eat better, and enhance our sex lives?

I live in Texas. One of our biggest annual celebrations is Cinco de Mayo. We have numerous parades and people enjoy a variety of Mexican beers and tequilas. One year I asked a number of partygoers if they knew what Cinco de Mayo was meant to commemorate. Overwhelmingly, the answer was Mexican Independence Day, which is wrong. Mexican independence is celebrated on September 16. Cinco de Mayo commemorates the Mexican army's unlikely victory over the French forces of Napoleon III on May 5, 1862, at the Battle of Puebla. As Americans, what we do know is that Cinco de Mayo is a day for excessive drinking. The same could be said for St. Patrick's Day. Green beer is the focus of the day, not the snakes being driven out of Ireland.

The evening news tends to skim over the trauma and violence that result from intoxicated behavior. It is usually when a sports figure or other celebrity is involved that the media pays attention. The truth is that it happens all of the time. A good friend of mine happens to be a Texas State District Judge who hears civil and family law cases. Although we rarely see stories about children being removed from their homes, or newborn babies testing positive for drug use, he deals with those situations every day. You can look at a district court calendar online in most large cities. Select a date and count how many drug-related cases are heard in your city. The media does us all a great injustice by not reporting more facts about drug addiction, accidental deaths, and suicide. Perhaps if they did, the actual statistics wouldn't seem so unbelievable.

This is not a wholesale condemnation or assault on our nation or our media; it is just a snapshot of the American culture. There is nothing wrong with alcohol in moderation, just as there is nothing wrong with many prescription drugs when they are used as directed. As Americans, we have become accustomed to using a pill to solve our problems and alcohol to celebrate our victories.

You may think this sounds ridiculous, but let me share some facts with you.

SOME FACTS ABOUT ADDICTION

Many new "wonder drugs" are released each year and far too often these new drugs tend to have unforeseen consequences. For instance, did you know that in 1888 the Bayer Pharmaceutical company released a new miracle drug named heroin? It was prescribed for everything from headaches to the common cold, and it was readily available in pre-loaded syringes through mail order catalogs.

According to the American Society of Addictive Medicine's Opioid Addiction 2016 Fact & Figures, drug overdose was the leading cause of accidental death in the United States in 2015, opioid addiction is driving this epidemic. Opioids are drugs made from opium and synthetic opiates that act as sedatives or narcotics; these include common pain medications like codeine and oxycodone, as well as heroin.

In 2012, there were 259 million prescriptions written for opioids, which is more than enough to give every American adult his own bottle of pills. Four out of five new heroin users started out misusing prescription painkillers.

Of this addicted population, there are alarming statistics for adolescents aged 12–17. In 2014, there were 467,000 adolescents who were current non-medical users of pain relievers. Most adolescents who misuse prescription pain relievers are given them for free by a friend or relative. In addition, the prescribing rates for opioids among adolescents and young adults nearly doubled between 1994 and 2007.

"The number of deaths by accidental drug overdose in

Texas is rising at an alarming rate. But many of the victims aren't your typical addicts: They're average people hooked on legal prescription drugs. "The majority are people with homes and families and jobs and, you know, just you or me," says Mary Beck, Chief Services and Evaluation Officer at the Council on Alcohol and Drugs, Houston.

Deaths from accidental overdoses increased in the state by more than 150 percent from 1999 to 2007, from 790 to 1,987, according to a recent report from the Drug Policy Alliance, a New York–based drug policy think tank. Accidental poisoning during that time was the third-leading cause of injury-related deaths statewide, behind only car crashes and suicide. "Texas is sort of like a microcosm for something happening all over the United States," says Meghan Ralston, Harm Reduction Coordinator for the Drug Policy Alliance."
-Texas Tribune, Brandi Grissom November 23, 2010

Being watchful for signs of drug and alcohol abuse in your own family is not being paranoid; it is sensible and realistic! For additional facts and figures on drug abuse refer to Appendix I on page 217.

THE DISEASE OF ADDICTION

We refer to addiction as a two-fold disease; it has mental and physical components.

The mental obsession is a deep-seated desire of every alcoholic and drug addict to be able to safely use as others do. We think we are different or we have a method to keep us safe. Most young adults do not believe they will ever get caught or overdose.

The mental obsession is powerful; it wins every time, and we use again and again. We become uncomfortable, angry, stressed out, or fearful. We find ourselves unable to cope as ordinary people do every day. The idea that something is wrong with us returns, and we begin to dwell on the negative rather than looking for solutions. In our minds, we have a tested solution that works every time. When things become overwhelming we go back to using.

This is the very reason so many people are resistant to treatment; somewhere deep inside they believe that they can control their addiction. Consider the following example.

You know a guy who is losing everything due to his drinking. He is about to lose his job, go to jail, lose his home, and lose his wife all because he is always drunk.

You see him at the bar getting as drunk as ever, and when you point out everything at stake and say "Here you are drinking," he may reply, "Yes! I'm so glad that you understand."

Of course, you do not understand it at all. It seems absurd and people are often offended by his total lack of control, but to him it makes perfect sense. With all the negativity and pending consequences over his head, it becomes too much to fathom and his only escape is to find that sense of ease and comfort in drinking or using.

The one thing that is causing him to lose everything is the very thing he feels he needs to survive.

This man could receive help and be able to overcome his

addiction. He could regain everything he has lost. On the other hand, if he continues to drink, he will certainly lose everything and eventually drink himself to death.

Unless he is offered hope and a way out, this miserable existence seems like a normal life to him. A normal life with bad luck, but to him it is the only life he understands.

As insane as it sounds, I can assure you that when we are active in our addiction it not only makes sense to use, but it feels like something we must do; it is normal. As our addiction grows, we discover the drugs' power and use them to help us forget or cope with our lives. We started out because we liked the way they made us feel, and over time we discovered their power to help us forget.

If you take away this coping mechanism without offering a real solution, an addict will soon find himself in a very dark place and in a downward spiral of thoughts.

It is when we feel as though we cannot live with it and we cannot live without it that hopelessness and despair begin to set in. We may ruin our family and find ourselves homeless or incarcerated. Eventually, we will drive away every person who cares about us and will start to feel as though the world would be better off without us. This is when we are at the greatest risk of taking our own lives.

This happens far more often than most people know. While we are using, we have a solution, and as miserable and chaotic as our lives may appear to others, we think it works for us.

The second part of addiction is the physical component.

We know that too much alcohol or drugs at any one time can cause an overdose and that prolonged substance abuse has long-term and significant health consequences. Once you remove car crashes and alcohol poisoning, alcoholics typically die for three different reasons: cirrhosis of the liver, pancreatic cancer, or a heart attack.

To better understand this, we need to look at the breakdown of alcohol in the body of an average non-alcoholic person.

Once a normal drinker introduces alcohol into his body, the pancreas and liver produce enzymes to break down the alcohol. Most alcohol is broken down, or metabolized, by an enzyme in the liver cells known as alcohol dehydrogenase (ADH). ADH breaks down alcohol into acetaldehyde (which has been linked to cancer), and then another enzyme, aldehyde dehydrogenase (ALDH), rapidly breaks down acetaldehyde into acetate. Acetate, or acetone, is what you find in nail polish remover. This information has been published by the Substance Abuse and Mental Health Services Administration (SAMHSA) and the National Institute on Alcohol Abuse and Alcoholism among others.

From this point, the remaining items are discharged from the body as carbon dioxide in our breath, water in our urine, and sugar into our blood. There are three methods used to test for intoxication or blood alcohol concentration (BAC): blood sample, breathalyzer, and urine analysis.

When dealing with an alcoholic, that process becomes dysfunctional. The pancreas and liver become unable to effectively process the amount of alcohol consumed because they no longer produce enough enzymes. For this reason, the breakdown process is much slower, and the alcohol remains as acetaldehyde for a prolonged period of time. In this form, it is three times as potent as the alcohol itself. When this occurs, the alcoholic feels as though he always needs one more, and will drink until he runs out, passes out, or is arrested. Why else would a relatively sane person drink all night and then decide to drive to the liquor store to buy more? He *believes* he needs just one more drink, or just a few more beers, and is willing to go to abnormal lengths to acquire those last few drinks. Heavily intoxicated people get behind the wheel to do this. There is an overwhelming compulsion to keep drinking, and our decision-making process was impaired much earlier in the night as we started drinking in excess. We call this the "phenomenon of craving." It is real and it has killed many of us, not to mention those who become victims of drunk driver automobile accidents.

Alcohol is an "ether-based" drug. Two other drugs that are ether-based are cocaine and methamphetamines. This may explain why so many alcoholics also like cocaine and meth. The opposite is also true; people on cocaine or meth often develop a problem with alcohol. The reason is quite simple: The body seeks the end result, which is ether, and it will quickly adapt to any delivery method.

Consider a man with a cocaine addiction who decided that once he completed treatment for cocaine he could drink a little. He claimed it was just to take the edge off and calm his nerves. He also said that he never had an issue with alcohol and could take it or leave it, but once his body broke down the alcohol, he quickly found himself unable to control his drinking. He asked why, but he did not like the answer and continued to drink.

Eventually, he had to face the fact that he was just as addicted to alcohol as he was to cocaine. In fact, he found that there were no safe drugs, not even marijuana. He had long ago passed over the threshold of controlling his drug usage, *any* drug usage. We call this cross-addiction, and it can jump from one family of drugs to another.

We may find that once we discover a new drug our bodies seem equipped to consume large amounts right from the start. We call this cross-tolerance. Cross-tolerance is a phenomenon that occurs when someone who is tolerant to the effects of one drug also develops a tolerance to another drug right away. It often happens between two drugs with similar functions or effects. An example would be two drugs that act on the same cell receptor or affect the transmission of certain neurotransmitters. This phenomenon can allow someone to become tolerant of a drug that he has never even used.

Tolerance is what changed within us between the day a 6-pack of beer would do us in for the night to the point where we could easily drink a 12-pack. Just as we have built up a tolerance to one drug, it is almost automatic for a different drug.

It is an addict's nature to want to experiment and swap one drug for another; there are a *multitude* to choose from. If addicts are ever to be completely free from the bonds of addiction, they are going to have to practice *total abstinence*. This means everything and anything that is habit forming, addictive, or changes how we feel. I'm not referring to antidepressants that target a chemical imbalance (though even the best of these will not work effectively if one is using other substances, including alcohol) but drugs for an effect that isn't "medical."

There are also medications designed to keep heroin addicts productive and free from opiate use. These include methadone and Suboxone. I am not a fan of these drugs or of the idea that drug replacement therapy is a good idea. Suboxone can be used for 5 to 10 days to help someone during an opiate detoxification process to minimize withdrawal symptoms, and it is very effective in that situation. But when it is used over a prolonged period of time, or as a "maintenance medication," it presents a whole new problem. Someone taking Suboxone for two years will have a future round of painful withdrawals to deal with. Many people become so ill that they turn back to street drugs for relief. Suboxone does not inhibit the use of other substances such as methamphetamine, cocaine, or benzodiazepines such as Xanax. Those combinations can be deadly. It is ameliorating only one aspect of a complex, multidimensional issue.

Another issue with medication maintenance is that when someone has been taking Suboxone or a similar opiate-antagonist medication for, let's say two years, his brain has not been efficiently producing dopamine since *before* starting drug therapy. Heroin and medications used for maintenance greatly impact the creation and release of dopamine in the brain by artificially triggering its release. Dopamine is a neurotransmitter that helps control the brain's reward and pleasure centers. Dopamine also helps regulate movement and emotional responses, and it enables us not only to see rewards, but to take action to move toward them. Dopamine deficiency results in Parkinson's disease, and people with low dopamine activity may be more prone to addiction. Long-term opiate and opiate-antagonist use leaves the brain unable to regulate its own production and release of the chemicals that allow us to feel pleasure and joy. Simply put, they can't "get happy."

Before you agree to an expensive drug replacement therapy for your child, consider this: Two years later your child is no longer in an inpatient setting where symptoms can be aggressively managed, and she will have to face the painful withdrawals and natural depression that come about due to the brain's failure to effectively produce dopamine. It will ultimately pass; however, it can be avoided from the beginning with a responsible detox to an abstinence protocol.

Methadone has been used in the United States since 1947 when it was approved for drug maintenance therapy due to its long half-life, which makes it an effective medication against the misery of opiate withdrawal. In most cases, methadone is a relatively inexpensive medication but often must be dispensed in the confines of a specially licensed clinic. This puts your child right back in the path of other people who may be actively using. Methadone clinics are unfortunately notorious places to find drugs or people who can find them for you. As a woman on my staff who was at the methadone maintenance clinic for more than six years said, "I always knew how to find drugs when I moved to a new city. I'd just find the methadone clinic." And in all of the years she worked in the clinic, she was never able to abstain from using heroin or other drugs. Both methadone and Suboxone are controversial, and the treatment industry is divided on the need or application for such drugs. I am a proponent of total abstinence. To be completely fair, I will say there are those who remain stable and productive on these drugs, but in my experience they are in the minority.

These drugs are widely available and their use is often encouraged, but I believe true freedom and recovery from addiction is found through abstinence. One thing is clear: Once an addiction develops, it will eventually kill the addict if left untreated, regardless of the substance. Until addicts are convinced that they can never use any mind-altering substance again, there is little hope of change and healing.

That is the crux of the problem and exactly what I will cover in the remaining chapters of this book.

ADDICTION AND JAIL

Getting in trouble with the law is a common element of addiction. We may be minding our own business when we catch the eye of a police officer. He notices we are intoxicated, and he arrests us for public intoxication. If we are arrested three times for the same offense, we may end up spending three to six months in the county jail. If we run, or lie about our identity, we could be charged with a more serious crime and spend much more time in jail.

If driving, we are charged with driving while intoxicated (DWI). Over the past few decades, this has become a much more serious crime: A car is a 4,000-pound bullet when driven by an intoxicated person. If we injure or kill someone, it becomes a felony and we may be looking at serious time in the penitentiary. If a child under the age of 15 is in our car, we will be charged with a felony that carries a two-year sentence for a first offense. If there is no other incident or injury but we are arrested for our third DWI, it is a felony.

Maybe we were stopped and had a prescription pill in our pocket. This too is a crime. Depending on the amount and the drug, we could be facing years in the penitentiary. It is easier than you may think to end up in a place designed for serious and violent criminals, just because we wanted to feel good.

In jail, our needs are met and contrary to what you may believe, as long as we do not look for trouble, we are much safer in jail. We have all seen the TV shows that lead us to believe there is constant chaos and violence, especially acts committed against young men and women entering the system for the first time. Although there is an element of truth to that in prison, in a county jail setting, much of it is hype.

Most people in our Denton County jail are placed in large residential areas called "pods." These pods house 48 men or women, with the bunks divided into two different areas separated by the TV area. Yes, a TV area. There is carpet, tables where they can eat or play cards, two different flat panel TVs with a variety of channels to watch, all supervised by a detention officer. An officer is always in the pod to answer questions, keep the peace, and aid inmates in a variety of ways. The pod is never left unsupervised. Doesn't sound so dangerous does it? There are also two classrooms to host a variety of meetings, services, or classes. One room has a washer and dryer, while the other has a game station like Xbox or PlayStation.

In the event someone does start trouble or a fight, it is broken up immediately and the aggressor is removed from the pod and placed in another section of the jail. Depending on the severity of their actions, they are either placed in a single cell or placed in an area referred to as barracks. This area looks like what we have all envisioned a jail to be: a concrete floor, steel furniture, and bars. I jokingly call it the old Gunsmoke jail because it reminds me of the old Western TV show about Marshal Dillon. Even this area is monitored and populated by men or women who share the same classification. (Classification is a method of assessing inmate risks that balance security requirements with program needs. Newly admitted inmates are assessed for risk and assigned a classification to determine where they will be housed.) Jail may not be fun, but it is far safer than we are led to believe.

Whether we are on the street or allowed back in our home, we *will* go out to find more drugs. This makes us susceptible to getting robbed at gunpoint, getting caught up in a drug deal gone bad, or experiencing an overdose where no one is around to call for help.

A famous musician, Nikki Sixx, the bassist for Mötley Crüe, overdosed from heroin in 1987. When the paramedics arrived, he was pronounced dead after his heart stopped beating for two minutes and was covered up in the back of the ambulance. A few minutes later, he somehow came to, pulled off the sheet covering his body, and ran away with the needle still hanging from his arm. He was so freaked out that he ran home. Once there, he was so shaken from what had happened that he could not calm down. He injected himself with more heroin. The next day he could not believe what he had done and realized that he was in real trouble. Today Nikki has been sober for years and says that sobriety is the greatest gift you will ever receive. He celebrates every year on his sober birthday.

While in jail, if we go into severe withdrawals, there is a nearby medical unit or hospital to which we can be transported. I have personally detoxed on the Dallas County jail room floor four times. It is not fun nor is it comfortable, but it is an experience that I will never forget. Some of the best sleep I ever had during my using career was while I was in the county jail.

Don't get me wrong; jail isn't what anyone hopes for their children. But addiction turns what we believe on its head; a county jail can be a good alternative to seeing a loved one using on the street.

It is shocking how many people end up in the penitentiary because they like to get high or drunk. A huge percentage of users fit into this category: nonviolent offenders who say they hurt no one but themselves. As parents, we cannot imagine our children ever doing something so heinous that they would end up in prison. The truth is, it is very easy to end up doing years in prison when our lifestyle includes drugs.

WHO IS AT RISK?

Before moving forward to the next chapter, let's debunk one more myth about addiction. Addiction can strike any family; it has nothing to do with how much you have, who you are or how well you have raised your kids.

This point is critical, so let me repeat it: Addiction has absolutely nothing to do with who you are or how well you have raised your children. This is not a moral failing.

People from all walks of life and every level of success are at risk. There is no race, religion, or career that has been granted immunity. I have yet to meet anyone who can honestly say there is no addiction in their entire extended family or place of employment. With a reported 10 to 12% of our population suffering from an addiction, it is this simple: If you know more than 10 people, you know an addict or an alcoholic. You may not realize it because addicts are very clever and can hide their addiction for a time, but they are there. According to the Texas Department of State Health Services, in 2000 about 16% of all Texas adults had a problem with alcohol and 5% had a problem with drugs.

We come in the form of politicians, pilots, clergy, teachers, housewives, business professionals, doctors, nurses, therapists, celebrities, bankers, police officers, fire/rescue personnel, financial advisors, lawyers, prison guards, scientists, inventors, students, siblings, parents, grandparents, and, of course, don't forget the kid selling dope on the corner. He is the one we want to point to as the real drug addict, but in reality, he is a very small percentage of the problem as a whole. In fact, I believe that he makes up the smallest percentage because his business is shut down as soon as it is discovered by law enforcement. Sure, there is another guy to take his place, but overall, there are far fewer of them than any of the others listed above.

I once called on a church to see if I could be of any help. They had a congregation of 3,000. I personally knew a handful of men and women within this congregation who suffered from an active addiction. When I offered to leave my contact information so that others could find me, I was told that there were no addicts or alcoholics at this church. Percentages told me that there would be at least 300, but I played along and said that he could take my information with him to give to his friends and coworkers who may need help. With a slightly sharper tone, I was told that this congregation did not associate with such people. Now I don't know if he had his head in the sand, or if it was more about not airing dirty laundry, but he was wrong, dead wrong, and I think he knew it. I know for a fact that there are families on his own staff who struggle with addiction, but I could see this conversation was going nowhere.

This is the problem for many of the families who need help the most. They refuse to see the truth or allow addicts to get any outside help because they feel it will reflect poorly on them.

DRUG ADDICTION AND SCIENTIFIC RESEARCH

The American Medical Association (AMA) declared that alcoholism was an illness in 1956. In 1991, the AMA further endorsed the dual classification of alcoholism by the International Classification of Diseases under both psychiatric and medical sections.

The United States National Library of Medicine has published the following information about drug addiction.

Drug addiction is a common brain disorder that is extremely costly to the individual and to society. Genetics contributes significantly to vulnerability to this disorder, but identification of susceptibility genes has been slow. Recent genome-wide linkage and association studies have implicated several regions and genes in addiction to various substances, including alcohol and, more recently, tobacco. Current efforts aim not only to replicate these findings in independent samples but also to determine the functional mechanisms of these genes and variants.

Addictions are chronic, often relapsing disorders characterized by obsession, compulsion, or physical or

psychological dependence. The World Health Organization estimates that there are 2 billion alcohol users, 1.3 billion tobacco users, and 185 million illicit-drug users worldwide. Twin and family studies provide strong evidence that addictions involve the interplay of genetic and environmental factors. Therefore, greater knowledge of the genetics underlying addiction is crucial for the development of more effective interventions."

-Nature Review Genetics April 2009, Ming D. Li Ph.D. and Margit Burmeister.

As I noted earlier, addiction has no boundaries and can strike any family, regardless of how educated, wealthy, or famous. We've all heard about the tragedies of River Phoenix, Jimi Hendrix, and Robin Williams. The following is a short list of people you may be familiar with but did *not know* struggled with addiction:

- Emily Dickinson
- Sylvia Plath
- Benjamin Franklin
- Sigmund Freud
- Vincent Van Gogh
- Charles Dickens
- Thomas Edison
- F. Scott Fitzgerald

- Marcus Aurelius
- Pope Leo XIII

Before we can address anything, we must first be willing to acknowledge it. The following chapters are designed to do just that. I will challenge you to look at family dynamics, actions, and surroundings in a different light. Some of what you will read may be uncomfortable, but I urge you to read on and finish the entire book before you decide that your situation is somehow different. The strength and perseverance needed to effectively deal with addiction within your own family may seem out of reach, but it is not. The clear-cut direction included in this book will change how you look at things and help you find the strength necessary to deal with this difficult situation.

HOW TO USE THIS BOOK

Each chapter builds on the information provided in the preceding chapter. I want to empower you through education and information. I implore you to read the chapters *as they are laid out,* not to just skip to the chapter title that speaks to you the loudest. The benefit of this book lies in its totality, so approach this the way you would approach a math textbook. You can't jump straight to Calculus without doing Pre-Algebra; likewise, you can't run head on into an intervention without doing the investigation and due diligence ahead of time.

Here is a brief overview of the following chapters:

Chapter 2 – What Drug Use Looks Like in the Home

Are my children at risk? Are they using in the

family home? Where are they hiding their drugs and drug paraphernalia? How can someone safeguard the family home? I address and answer these questions and more, offering families step-by-step guidance that is informed by both my personal and professional experiences.

.

Chapter 3 – What Are Some of My Options?

Now that we have a better understanding of both addiction and what drug use in the home looks like, what shall we do with all of this information? This chapter presents a number of options and recommendations. This information will help you make an educated decision about what needs to happen next.

Chapter 4 – The Legal Community

Whether your child has had contact with law enforcement or not, you will want to read this chapter thoroughly. Understanding how the legal community can be one of your greatest resources will give you additional tools to fight the addiction, while providing hope and security for the entire family. If your child is using, it is just a matter of time until the police or Child Protective Services shows up at your door. You will learn how to navigate these events and position yourself for the best possible outcome.

Chapter 5 – The Intervention

This chapter provides a step-by-step roadmap to planning and participating in an intervention.

This will be one of the most difficult tasks you will ever have to carry out. Understanding how to work with the interventionist instead of hampering his efforts is the key to successful interventions. Many families attempt such tasks on their own; however, few are able to clearly see the correct path and actions.

Chapter 6 – Treating the Addiction

In this chapter, I present an in-depth look at the treatment process from beginning to end. You will learn how to make an informed selection and maximize the chance for better outcomes as you gain knowledge about treatment specialties, associated costs, insurance, and aftercare.

Chapter 7 – Getting Out of the Way: The Most Dangerous Time

Here you will learn what to do and what not to do, when to act and when to let go. Providing services at this crucial time is where I started my career. This is when our actions have more to do with the success of the addicted loved one than anything else. As a family, we have the power to help or harm the addicted loved one's recovery; without informed direction, it can be a recipe for disaster.

Chapter 8 – What Life Should Look Like in Long-Term Recovery

This is the payoff for all of the hard work,

planning, self-evaluating, and action you have taken up to this point. This chapter will help you know when your child is on steady ground and when he is not. When all is well, you will experience a better relationship with your child than ever before. After reading this chapter, if you see troubling behaviors, you will know how to respond to those red flags and handle possible situations.

Chapter 9 – A Personal View

This chapter highlights my journey through addiction and recovery. From the stage to a jail cell and back, my family and I have weathered this storm, finding every pitfall and making bad decisions along the way. I have walked through more than most, which has prepared me for a career in addiction and recovery. Everything I do is to keep people out of the ground and able to find true happiness and meaningful careers. This book is the culmination of all my experiences, including over 21 years of working with others.

CHAPTER TWO

WHAT DRUG USE LOOKS LIKE IN THE HOME

Now that we have learned something about the physical and mental aspects of addiction, we need to look within our own home. In order to get a complete picture of what is really going on, we must look at each component of our child's life under our own roof.

There exists a small, unsettling feeling in the pit of our stomach; could our child be using drugs? We feel it. It's the thought that keeps us up at night, but we don't want to say it out loud, and certainly not in front of others. We will deny it and then deny it again, but we know. The signs are there.

CONFIRMING SUSPICIONS

Think about teenagers and what you know about them. They can be moody, erratic, secretive, unpleasant, and irrational. Their wardrobe, taste in music, and friends may change overnight. They may lose interest in ideas and activities that were once important to them. Their schoolwork may suffer and they may abandon the idea of going to college. These are the signs parents are told to look for, and yet these could just be signs that you are dealing with a moody teenager, tween, or young adult. Any sudden or drastic change may be a sign of drug or alcohol use, or it could just be driven by raging hormones and a desire to fit in. I would say that at some point almost all of us have made a drastic and sudden change to seem more appealing to someone we are attracted to or a group we wanted to be a part of.

Here is the best advice I can offer. If you think something is wrong with your teenager, give her a drug test. Yes, she will be angry and say things like, "I thought you trusted me!" Here is the answer you need to give: "I love you too much to not do this." Afterwards, let her be mad, call you names, and throw a fit. One day she will probably thank you for caring enough to make sure she was safe; until then, you need to grow some thick skin. This is not a one-time event. Test her randomly with different types of tests. Go to a lab that has experience with drug screening employees and applicants. These businesses will have the latest technology needed to identify the constantly changing synthetic designer drugs as well as common street drugs. There are oral swabs, urinalysis, and skin patches; it is a good idea to change up the methodology.

Keep in mind that there is a drug testing facility within miles of every hospital. Pull out your phone, open a mapping app, and type in "Drug Testing" or "Lab." My guess is that you will find a number of choices. If you live in a large city, many of these choices will be within a few miles of your home. There are five labs within five minutes of my home.

You may even tell your teenager that you read an article about kids on drugs and mention that you might start drug testing to ensure the safety of your home. A few days later take a look around her room, closet, and bathroom to see if there are any supplements, cleanses, or "flushes" used to circumvent or beat drug tests.

There is a multimillion dollar industry dedicated to passing drug tests. They sell a variety of supplements, fake urine, and products like the "Whizzinator." The original Whizzinator is a product intended to fraudulently defeat drug tests. The Whizzinator comes as a kit complete with dried urine, a syringe, heater packs (to keep the urine at body temperature), a false penis available in several skin tones, and an instruction manual. The company also offered a female version of the Whizzinator, called "Number One."

There are many different types of products like this, so if you find something you are not sure of, take a picture of it and show it to someone who might know. If you have a friend who has dealt with this in his home, show him the picture. If you don't ask, you don't know. If you do not know anyone who can help, Google "beat drug tests" and look at the different images to see if they match what you have found. If you confront your child and he says it is for something entirely different, Google that and see what you can learn. Google is an endless source of information, so utilize it.

We want to work with facts from now on, and drug testing is the first fact to gather. Your child is either clean or he is testing positive for one or more drugs.

Fact.

A good strategy is to test your child again just a day or two after a drug test. Many people feel as though the safest time to use is the next day or even later the very same day that they passed a test. Many of the drugs available leave the body within 72 hours, so anyone with a reasonable ability to stop using or utilize deceptive screening products can regularly beat a drug test. Eventually, your child will not be able to keep this up as her addiction takes a firm grip; however, we are talking about catching our children while they are experimenting and have not yet developed a full-blown addiction.

Other items you may find are heavy-duty foil, burnt foil, burnt and bent spoons, cotton balls, eye drops, rubbing alcohol, candles, air freshener, syringes, plastic bags, hollowed out writing pens, scales, soda cans, and small vials to name just a few. You might find a substance in a small plastic bag or foil. Again, take a picture and call someone who might know about these things.

You will have to really look for evidence of drug and alcohol use because when we use we hide things. Start with your child's room and look around for things that are out of place. This includes checking the closet and bathroom.

Other places to look are inside speakers, cabinets, ornate boxes, backpacks, and personal bags; between mattresses; under the bed; above tall shelves and furniture; in the toilet tank; and under loose floorboards, rugs, and loose carpet in corners of all rooms where your kids hang out. These places include the attic, the garage, sheds, and all cars. Then take your search a step further. You were a child once. Where did you hide things? In the air return vent? Do you have any pills or liquor that is not securely locked up? Have you recently checked for unauthorized consumption? Do you monitor medications for your child? Are you sure he is not trading medications for other drugs?

Pick a day when your child is away at school or other activity and search every inch of his space. If you put everything back in its place, he will not know you have searched. If you find something like a dirty magazine or other slightly disturbing or offensive material, put it back. If you feel you must confront him, do so; however, you have found his hiding place, and if you let the small stuff slide, you can periodically check for other items he may hide. If you confront him about a dirty magazine or video, you have alerted him to the fact that you are searching and discovered his hiding place(s). I do not wish to minimize or offend your thoughts on such matters as pornography; to confront or not is a decision you must make according to your own beliefs on the subject. You must choose your battles. I will say that sometimes the police let lesser crimes go or choose not to bring someone in on a warrant for a minor offense in order to catch the person in question committing a much more serious crime. For example, if the officer knows someone has a little weed on him but believes he is on his way to buy more, he may let the small amount go in order to catch both the dealer and buyer at a later time. This may be a time to utilize a similar plan of attack.

If your child is experimenting, chances are he keeps the drugs on him at all times. You will need to decide when it is appropriate to have him empty out all of his pockets, socks, etc. If you are going to search him, search him all the way. Hand him a robe or other outfit and have him remove his clothes in front of you. (Otherwise he will get rid of anything he has.) When he objects, let him know that this is much easier than having a full cavity search at the county jail if he got caught with any illegal substance. These are not just scare tactics; this is what really happens in jail.

As a teenager, when smoking pot, I always kept the bag stashed in my underwear in the front just below my belt. Rolling papers were in my wallet and small pipes were in my pockets or the ashtray of my car. I often hid things in my pack of cigarettes, but today smoking is not as fashionable. Teenagers use vapes (electronic cigarettes) and you can put almost anything in a vape. Vape oil or e-juice is a liquid that is heated up and then inhaled. Police are finding all kinds of drugs in these devices, so if you are unsure get the fluid tested at a lab. You may be ridiculed, especially if it turns out to be nothing more than the legal e-juice sold in vape stores. But what is more important? That you were wrong and possibly looked foolish, or the fact that you took measures to ensure the safety of your family? Again, later in life your teenagers probably will thank you for caring. I do not apologize for checking and my kids knew I would call the police if needed. They all acted offended and said I was ridiculous for testing them, but I knew what was real and what was suspicion.

I have a blended family with three children from different fathers. One of them has been to jail and treatment, another dabbled for a while and decided that the consequences and trouble were not worth it, and the youngest stayed completely away from all drugs and alcohol. They all know my past and have seen a number of family members suffer from addiction, go to jail, and die. We have never shielded them from the truth about these things and I believe they are all thankful for how we dealt with this subject. Now I can tell you that all three of them were appalled when I tested them for drugs. Addiction can strike any family, especially when it runs through your family tree.

One idea you must wrap your mind around is the absolute medical fact that many of us are genetically predisposed to developing an addiction. This does not mean you have bad genes or that all of your kids are going to be addicts because your uncle, father, and cousin are. Addiction skips through the family tree with no real rhyme or reason. I have it but my siblings do not. My mother and all seven of her siblings and their spouses do not have any addiction issues; however, my cousins are a different story. In several families there was a child just like me. Most of my cousins are fine, but a handful of us were not. One of my cousins passed away a number of years ago from a drug overdose. So whose fault is it? Who caused my cousins and me to become addicts and alcoholics? There were not many families as strait-laced as my mother's family. My grandfather was the sheriff, and no drugs or alcohol ever entered their home. We don't know why it skips around from one generation to the next; we just know that any family is susceptible. We also know that just because both parents have an addiction does not mean their children will.

You will not catch everything, but if you are diligent and your children know where you stand, your family home will remain safer than the average home in your neighborhood. If you are going out of town, take extra measures to ensure your house will not become the big party venue of the year. Alert your neighbors. Do not leave teenagers alone in the home. Set up a security system. With today's technology, you can place a number of high definition cameras in and around your home for a very reasonable price. These new cameras record video and sound anytime there is movement. The majority of them offer night vision and a subscription that keeps all files for 10 to 30 days. They alert you anytime there is a power outage or the cameras go offline for any reason. Even if your child enters the room and unplugs the camera, you will be alerted via text or email and be able to watch him approach the camera and grab the cord.

HOW SOMEONE LOOKS AND ACTS WHILE USING DIFFERENT DRUGS

It is helpful to know the telltale signs of drug use. In this section, I describe the signs and behaviors associated with the most commonly used drugs.

Alcohol – When people are drunk, it's pretty easy to tell if you know what to look for. As they become intoxicated, the very first thing altered is good judgment. This alone is not always easy to spot, as teenagers and young adults often don't exercise good judgment. Judgment is controlled by the cerebrum, which is the largest portion of our brain. It is composed of right and left hemispheres and performs higher functions like interpreting touch, vision, and hearing, as well as speech, reasoning, emotions, learning, and fine control of movement. When sound reasoning is compromised, people often make bad decisions, such as driving after drinking too much.

The next system to be impaired is motor skills, which is controlled by the cerebellum. Its function is to coordinate muscle movements and maintain posture and balance.

Once this system is affected, symptoms can include slurred speech, lack of steadiness, and loss of balance. This is why law enforcement uses roadside tests for intoxication, such as walking a straight line or reciting the alphabet. The more intoxicated someone is, the easier it is to spot.

Continued drinking will affect the vital functions center known as the brainstem. It consists of the medulla oblongata, pons, and midbrain, and continues downward to form the spinal cord. Here is where automatic functions take place, such as breathing, heart rate, body temperature, wake and sleep cycles, digestion, sneezing, coughing, vomiting, and swallowing. When this system is compromised, there is a risk of death. I'm sure you have seen stories on the news of college students who drank so much they died.

They call it alcohol poisoning and it occurs when large amounts of alcohol are consumed, like at a keg party where people are using a beer bong. A beer bong is a large funnel with a short hose attached. One or more beers are poured in the large opening of the funnel while keeping your thumb against the end of the hose to keep the beer from running out. Once the hose is at the mouth, the thumb is removed, and in less than one second, one or more beers flow down your throat and into your stomach.

Stimulants (Speed, Meth, Cocaine, and ADD Meds) – When someone is using stimulants, there are a number of physical signs to look for; one or more could mean your child is using speed. This includes abusing Attention Deficit Disorder (ADD) meds, such as Ritalin, Adderall, Vyvance, Dexedrine, Concerta, Daytrana, Focalin, and Adzenys.

- **Excessive Sweating** – Even if it's cool outside or a user is just sitting still, she has copious sweat pouring down her forehead, covering her face, and soaking her clothes, especially around her armpits. She may look as though she has been performing heavy manual labor outside in temperatures exceeding 100 degrees, and yet she is doing nothing more than watching television.
- **Dilated Eyes/Pupils** – Anytime your child's eyes are dilated, you can bet there is something amiss. It will be difficult to see in a dark room, so if you are concerned, turn on the light and make eye contact.
- **Nervous Twitch** – Your child may be unable to stay completely still and not fidget. You may notice that she rubs her nose, touches items multiple times, or makes facial gestures while speaking.
- **Paranoid** – Fear of being chased, or that everything will implode, despite all rational evidence, is a sign that your child is abusing stimulants.
- **Tinkering or Excessive Cleaning ("Geeking")** – Examples of this behavior include cleaning at all hours of the night or performing chores like cleaning window blinds one blade at a time. You may also see your child picking through the carpet or checking each and every item on the floor, searching for drugs they may have dropped. Another common activity is disassembling small motors or electronic devices and rarely ever putting them back together. These behaviors are often seen with stimulant use.
- **Pasty Mouth** – People who use stimulants often develop a dry or "pasty" mouth that causes them

to continuously lick their lips, smack their lips, and force swallows while trying to talk.

- **Ramble On** – A user often talks a mile a minute, running on and on and making little sense. Stimulants can also cause muscle tightness or spasms that make it difficult to speak coherently or control the movement of their jaw and mouth.
- **Lack of Sleep** –You may observe your loved one staying up all night, pacing, tossing and turning. Stimulants make falling asleep extremely difficult, even 10 or 12 hours after the last use. Once a user does fall asleep, he may sleep for days and be difficult to rouse. Those "geeking" sessions can take place at any hour of the night or early morning. Regular hours have little meaning or relevance.
- **Loss of Appetite** – Sudden weight loss or inability or disinterest in eating could be signs of stimulant use. If your child usually eats an entire pizza but finds it difficult just to eat a handful of crackers, combined with some of the other behaviors mentioned, that can be a definite red flag.
- **Heart Rate** – When using stimulants, a user's heart is almost always racing. This happens even when she should be relaxed. Large amounts of any stimulant will cause the heart rate to increase, sometimes to very dangerous levels.

Opiates and Benzos – Opiates are drugs made from both opium and synthetic opiates, including Vicodin, Morphine, Codeine, Oxycodone, Oxycontin, Percocet, Dilaudid, Fentanyl, Lortab, Demerol, Hydrocodone, Methadone, Suboxone, Subutext, and heroin.

Benzodiazepines are a type of medication known as

tranquilizers. Familiar names include Valium, Klonopin, Ativan, and Xanax; however, this family of drugs includes many more names. Legitimate reasons for prescribing a "benzo" would be to treat anxiety, insomnia, or alcohol withdrawal; for anti-seizure control; and for muscle relaxation.

I grouped these two types of drugs together because they often present some of the same characteristics or behaviors. This is because they are both depressants. This means that one or more of the following symptoms may be present:

- **Nodding Off** – This happens when someone is on the verge of losing consciousness. Much like the term, it is when the head starts to dip or nod, and the person looks as though he is falling asleep. This may happen while talking, eating, or, most dangerously, driving. He is not sleeping. He is losing consciousness and it is extremely dangerous. This indicates that the vital function center of his brain is affected. One who loses consciousness is at great risk of aspirating, slipping into a comatose state, or fatally overdosing.

- **Excessive Sleeping** – Sleeping late may mean that your child has been staying up too late on occasion, but sleeping all of the time is a different matter. Something is wrong and your first move should be a drug test. If he is in fact clean, he should see a doctor, as young people should not sleep all of the time. If he is staying up all night every night, that too should be addressed.

- **"Pinned" Eyes/Constricted Pupils** – Opiates impact the parasympathetic nervous system that controls this reflex. When we are in a dark room, our pupils dilate to let in as much light as possible and then shrink or constrict when light is introduced. This reaction is diminished by opiate use.

- **Itchiness** – Some people cannot stop itching when they are using opiates or benzos. Opiates in particular cause a release of histamines. A user may be constantly touching his face or rubbing his nose raw.
- **Constipation** – Have you seen one of the new commercials advertising medication for opiate-induced constipation? Opiate abuse is now so rampant in our society that it gets its very own category of constipation, with ads for medications to fix it. I don't know whether to laugh or cry. Opiates slow the bowels and affect relevant muscles, which is why so many people using opiates are often constipated. Look for opiate- induced constipation medications or laxatives.

Other Drugs – The following is a list of symptoms that may be caused by any number of different drugs. Again, if you are not certain, you should test your child for drug use.

- **Irritable** – Personality or mood changes may be caused by a number of issues; however, they are also associated with drug use, so you will want to investigate to determine the cause.
- **Eyes (Red, Pinned, or Dilated)** – You know what your child's eyes look like, so you should be able to spot when her eyes just don't look right.
- **Avoidance** – This is huge and is almost always present with all drugs or alcohol. Your child

shows up at home, says she's home, and quickly walks to her room or somewhere, *anywhere,* in the house that you are not. As easy as it is to write this off as a moody teenager move, you want to make better contact. Even if she has friends over, walk into the room they're in and turn the lights on. Look them all in the eyes and ask a few questions, such as "How are you all doing tonight?" or "What have you guys been up to? Did you have a good time?" It doesn't really matter what the questions are. Look for eye contact, speech patterns, eye movement while talking, steadiness of balance, and the ability to answer questions in a forthright manner. These are signs that all systems of the brain are correctly working and are not impaired. We don't need to make a scene. The kids will know that you always want to see them and talk with them when they get home. Teenagers and young adults are already difficult to communicate with, so opening a new mandatory line of communication is good and healthy on a number of levels.

- **Always Gone** – When kids are high, they will go to great lengths to stay out of their parents' way. It is much easier to just stay away. It goes along with avoidance. If your child is spending an inordinate amount of time away from home, you need to find out *why.* If your child is spending the night at a friend's home, call and confirm that the parents are aware. It will clear things up if they were told that the children were staying at *your* house—an old trick to get a free night out without any parental supervision. This is yet another time to insert yourself. With consistency, this will be second nature and expected by your children. They count on your involvement and it will dissuade them from that type of behavior.

- **Personality Change** – Remember that children, especially teenagers, will experience personality changes while finding where they fit within the complex social make-up of their school. A sudden personality change is a great time to open up a conversation about school and what's going on. Again, you are learning much more than the questions asked and answered. You are looking at nonverbal communication: Are they turning away from us, avoiding eye contact, looking down, or fidgeting? What do you notice about their speech patterns? What do their responses tell you about their reasoning skills? All of this unspoken communication tells us more than words ever will.

INITIAL RESPONSE TO THE DISCOVERY OF DRUGS OR ALCOHOL

Let's say you know your child is intoxicated and you have confronted her. I recommend that once you establish she is using you give her a drug test and collect her phone. Send her to bed, provided she is steady on her feet and is not testing positive for opiates. You may even say that how she conducts herself over the next few minutes will determine how long it will be before her phone is returned. If you are concerned about the level of intoxication, *do not hesitate* to take her to the ER to have her checked out.

Nothing meaningful can be accomplished while your child is intoxicated and you are in the heat of the moment. The next day, when you are not overly emotional, and your child is clear minded, tell her what the consequences are and establish the protocol for drug testing. At this time, your teenager should not be allowed to drive and must submit to restricted activities. If the problem persists despite your conversations and consequences, it may be time to elevate the stakes.

This is probably the last thing you want to hear, but *consider calling the police.* I know this is difficult, but it could save a life. If you have other children in the house, especially small children, you must keep them safe. The consequences could be catastrophic. People who are impaired leave things around. Small children get into everything. This is a dangerous combination. They can be exposed to and accidentally ingest a harmful substance. They can become sick or nonresponsive, and, of course, you would take them to the hospital. The hospital will do a drug screen as a matter of diagnostic procedure. If the results are positive, you will find yourself in a situation that defies imagination. Child Protective Services (CPS) and the police may come to your house and arrest *you.* They can take your children into protective custody while the state seeks temporary or permanent placement for all of your children. All the authorities know is that whatever your child ingested was in *your home and you failed to keep him safe.* Those are the facts they will act on. They will move to protect the children in the home and rightly so; it's what they're supposed to do. Hard to believe? Yes. But it has happened to good families who never imagined that this could happen, especially in their home.

Once this scenario starts, it is very challenging to maneuver. It can require significant resources, result in time missed from work and family, and involve long-lasting consequences. The children will never forget. Even if it is proven that your teen is at fault, you are still on the hook. If authorities can prove you had prior knowledge, then your reality has just changed forever; you could be charged with a felony. And the damage done to your family will last for years.

You really do not have a choice when it comes to this; you must take immediate action. Your child has not just placed himself at risk, he has put the entire family at risk. He will never see it this way and will claim you are overreacting, but you are the parent and he is the child. Teenagers have little knowledge of how the world works. Remember when you were a teenager and thought you knew so much more than you actually did? I remember looking at my dad as a child; in my eyes he could do no wrong. But as a teenager I wondered how this man was able to keep us all alive and fed. As an adult, I see how little I knew and thank God every day for the wisdom and strength my father has.

Other than drug and alcohol testing, you need to talk to your kids and ask them point blank about experimenting with either drugs or alcohol. Tell them the dangers of addiction and how you would deal with them if they were to start experimenting. In many homes, there is no question: If drugs or alcohol are found, the police are called.

In other homes, parents feel that if their kids are going to use, they should use in the safety of their own home. This is a *monumentally* bad idea which, again, may eventually lead to the arrest of both you and your child. From time to time, we see this on the news where parents are charged with a number of violations that may carry actual prison time. If a minor overdoses in your home, you can be held criminally responsible. Another possibility is that the parents of other children may file a lawsuit against you for allowing their child to be exposed to drugs or alcohol in your home. Parents who provide a home where their child can "safely use" often have no idea their children are bringing friends into the home. In either case, *you are responsible* and you will lose. Imagine the media at your front door, dragging your entire family through the mud. This can happen for two reasons. One, you were afraid to ask for help when you found something you knew was wrong. Two, you made the decision that it was okay for your child to drink or use drugs as long as he did it at home.

The problem with this is that once you allow your child to have a beer in the home, to him it is a green light to smoke pot or experiment with harder drugs. I grew up knowing such families and I can tell you that we always pushed the limits. No child allowed to use in the family home will follow the guidelines set forth. Responsible underage drinking is an oxymoron; there is no such thing.

The following is excerpted from a CNN report from 2014 and demonstrates how quickly things can happen and how powerless you can be; there are consequences for the entire family.

The rare moments Mr. Smith (name has been changed) can take a break from running his own painting business, he can be found toiling away on his family's dream house in the suburbs of Philadelphia.

"I'm a working guy. I work every day, six days a week, even seven if I have to," Smith says. One day this past March, without warning, the government took his house away, even though he and his wife have never been charged with a crime or accused of any wrongdoing.

"I was so upset thinking somebody's going to take my house for nothing. That makes me crazy," Smith says, shaking his head.

The nightmare began when police showed up at the house and arrested their 22-year-old son, on drug charges—$40 worth of heroin. Authorities say he was selling drugs out of the home. The Smiths say they had no knowledge of any involvement their son might have had with drugs.

A month-and-a-half later police came back—this time to seize their house, forcing the Smiths and their children out on the street that day. Authorities came with the electric company in tow to turn off the power and even began locking the doors with screws, the Smiths say. Authorities won't comment on the exact circumstances because of pending litigation regarding the case.

Police and prosecutors came armed with a lawsuit against the house itself. It was being forfeited and transferred to the custody of the Philadelphia District Attorney. Authorities said the house was tied to illegal drugs and therefore subject to civil forfeiture.

In two years, nearly 500 families in Philadelphia had their homes or cars taken away by city officials, according to records from Pennsylvania's attorney general. Authorities use a civil forfeiture law that allows them to seize people's property when that property is connected to the sale of illegal drugs. – CNN, September 2014

Civil Forfeiture in the United States, sometimes called Civil Judicial Forfeiture or occasionally Civil Seizure, is a controversial legal process that allows law enforcement officers to take assets from persons suspected of involvement with crime or illegal activity without necessarily charging the owners with wrongdoing.

As evidence of how wide ranging the consequences of civil forfeiture can be, consider the following quote from Richard Thornburgh, who served as Attorney General during Ronald Reagan's presidency:

"It's now possible for a drug dealer to serve time in a forfeiture-financed prison after being arrested by agents driving a forfeiture-provided automobile while working in a forfeiture-funded sting operation."

WHAT ARE SOME OF MY OPTIONS?

You now have a better understanding of addiction and what drug use in the home looks like. What will you do with all of this information? There are a number of possibilities. However, treating addiction can be very expensive and time-consuming. No one is "fixed" in 28 days. That is a myth. There must be an ongoing system of support and a drastic change in lifestyle and behavior if someone is to overcome his addiction and thrive. Keep reminding yourself that this is the goal: a meaningful life free from addiction.

WHAT IF MY CHILD IS PHYSICALLY SICK FROM WITHDRAWAL?

Sometimes a medical detox is required to safely remove all of the drugs and alcohol from the body. There are some substances, like alcohol or benzodiazepines, that can be deadly if detox doesn't happen in a responsible, medically supervised setting. Other drugs, like heroin and opiates, the painkiller class of medications, can cause painful withdrawal symptoms. The fear of that withdrawal is what drives many addicts to keep using. A medically managed detox protocol can address this. An addict's best chance in these situations is an inpatient detox in a medical facility. A medically supervised detox will usually cost between $5,000 and $8,000. If you have insurance coverage, you will want to use it.

WHY MIGHT SOMEONE NEED TO GO TO TREATMENT?

Not everyone needs to go to inpatient treatment, although most do. It can be helpful to work with a professional interventionist or engage the services of a clinician who can make an assessment and help make that determination. Here are some reasons treatment may be the right option:

1. The emotional pull of the street can be strong. The separation from our using buddies, peers, home, family, and the daily grind of life allows for an opportunity to focus solely on getting well.

2. Treatment centers employ a number of doctors and clinicians to help patients stabilize and see things in a new light. Through participation in group meetings, educational workshops, and seminars that explain addiction and recovery, there can be learning without the distractions of phones or social media. This time can also be useful in identifying "co-occurring disorders" such as depression or bipolar disorder.

3. Treatment centers often offer a family program that brings everyone to the table to talk about

things that can be difficult and emotional. The assistance of a trained therapist is very beneficial in these situations. It also arms the family with information and guidance.

4. If someone is strung out and knows he will face painful, frightening withdrawals, he can't do it on his own. When the withdrawals get bad enough, he will leave and get high just to feel better. We call this being "dopesick" and we will do almost anything to avoid that. It isn't just about comfort; often a medical detox is required to safely remove all of the drugs and alcohol from our bodies. Medical detox becomes a necessity as many combinations of drugs and alcohol can cause dangerous seizures.

5. If there are other disorders present, they must be treated as well as the addiction in order for someone to achieve permanent recovery. When two different disorders occur together, they should be treated together.

WHOM CAN I CALL?

You can always start out by calling a hotline for a drug prevention organization, such as the Partnership for Drug-Free Kids or the Drug Free America Foundation. Most states have a "drug hotline." The Texas Department of State Health Services number is 877-9-NO DRUG. There are a number of free services to help you that are not directly connected to any particular treatment center. You may need to make more than one call until you find someone who can answer your questions and provide a list of resources that meet your needs. The internet is also a useful source of information.

Another option is to a call a police department that

employs a family resource officer. You can call and ask for directions without having your child arrested. If you live in a small town or your local police force does not have such a position, try calling police departments in other cities within your state; each state has resources that others may not. I believe this person will try to help you.

Another great resource is criminal defense attorneys who handle drug cases. They deal with addiction every day and are usually aware of local resources. Your county should have a Bar Association with an online listing of lawyers, searchable by name or area of practice. Select Criminal Defense. There should also be a state Bar Association searchable by name, city, and areas of practice. My organization receives dozens of these types of calls on a daily basis.

WHAT IF I THINK MY KID HAS A CO-OCCURRING DISORDER?

"I don't know for sure, but it sure seems as though there is something else going on. He is always so moody and just wants to be left alone. It's not normal."

If you're not sure about this, I would recommend that you call a local clinician and describe what you are seeing. If you do not know how to find a qualified counselor in your area, I suggest PsychologyToday.com. Here you can sort clinicians by areas of expertise, experience, and location. I recommend you select someone with multiple years of experience who specializes in addiction and co-occurring disorders. In a large city, you will have many to choose from.

Once you make the call, ask if the counselor is well

acquainted with addiction and co-occurring disorders. Ask her if she has time for a consultation and what the charges would be for an assessment of any co-occurring disorders. This may cost between $100 and $300. This will inform you about what you are dealing with; the clinician should make recommendations for an appropriate level of care and facility.

WHAT DOES "LEVEL OF CARE" MEAN?

"Level of care" is a term used to indicate whether someone needs an inpatient residential treatment center (RTC), a partial hospitalization program (PHP), or an intensive outpatient program (IOP). An appropriate level of care is recommended based on the severity of an issue, how long someone has been using, and how long it has been since their last use. The idea here is to match the level of care with someone's level of need. Insurance companies will use the same markers to determine "medical necessity," which will dictate what they will pay and for how long, even if a program is "in network."

CAN I JUST CALL A TREATMENT CENTER AND GET MY KID IN TREATMENT?

Yes, you can, but let me ask a few questions. Is the treatment center you plan on calling one you saw in a TV commercial? Have you researched their expertise and out-of-pocket expenses? Do you understand what the out-of-pocket costs will be *even if they're in network with your insurance?* You can call a treatment center directly if the answers to those questions match up with your needs. If they don't, take some time to find a better fit.

There are a lot of treatment centers out there, *a lot.* Just because they have great commercials and a super slick website does not mean they are your best choices. Like any other industry, there are some companies that are not very helpful. Before calling a particular center, do a little research. See if there are any lawsuits or reckless charges you should be aware of. Find out what the total cost for services is and what insurance policies they accept.

If you are certain of these facts, or if a clinician you trust has recommended a facility, give them a call. I give these cautions because once you call a center, they may do their utmost to convince you that they are the right center for your needs. I am skeptical of late-night ads for treatment, especially those that claim cures or do not utilize a 12-step model. This is my opinion based on my experience. I believe in the old referral system, where the recommendations are based on your needs rather than quotas. Most clinicians and interventionists have a list of treatment centers they know and trust. We have met the staff and walked the grounds. We know what their areas of expertise are and we know the cost of treatment. We do our best to refer families to centers that meet their needs, both financially and in area of expertise.

SHOULD I CALL MY INSURANCE COMPANY BEFORE I CALL A TREATMENT CENTER?

Calling your own insurance company is a great idea. You will need to ask what kind of coverage you have, including aftercare, and which providers are in network. You will want to know what your out-of-pocket expenses are. Once you have a list of treatment centers in network with your policy, you can start your selection process with a better chance of knowing what your financial exposure will be. If you know these facts first, you can make a more informed selection. Ask the clinician or interventionist about the different centers on the list provided by your insurance company.

When speaking to a treatment center, make sure you are clear about out-of-pocket expenses. Ask them if they intend to use any of your aftercare benefits. Sometimes a treatment center will use your inpatient and aftercare benefits to keep someone in treatment as long as possible. The problem with this is that aftercare is a *crucial* part of the treatment process, and those benefits are intended for that specific level of care. Returning home, going back to work, and transitioning back into life is a delicate time in early recovery; the step down into a supportive intensive outpatient program, commonly known as an IOP, can ease that transition. If your benefits are prematurely used, it could cause an unexpected financial hardship. What usually happens is that the family chooses to forego aftercare and the addicted loved one is put at great risk of relapse.

If you are fully informed about your coverage and out-of-pocket expenses you will not be unpleasantly surprised when you are asked for more money, but you must make this clear to both your insurance company and the treatment center. A great question to ask is how many days they can typically get coverage for. A lot of insurance companies are approving only 12 to 14 days at the inpatient level of care, despite it being a 28-day program, based on what they deem *medically* necessary. "Medical necessity" is a hot topic in the insurance world, particularly with behavioral health where conditions labeled "life threatening" and "medically necessary" are not necessarily recognized past the initial crisis. Medical necessity based on insurance standards diminishes the longer someone has been clean, even in a treatment setting. This allows your insurance company to stop paying, even though the treatment is incomplete. Ask the treatment center what they will do in this case. Will they automatically go for your aftercare benefits (PHP and IOP), or will they ask you to pay the difference? At the time of admission, you may be told it will cost $5,000 to cover your deductible. If insurance fails to cover all 28 days, will they honor the price you were quoted, ask for more money, or utilize your aftercare benefits? You need to ask these questions up front because most people don't realize this can be an issue.

WHAT EXACTLY DOES MY INSURANCE COVER?

Some policies are better than others. An HMO is more affordable with less coverage and more restrictions. A PPO is more flexible with better coverage, but it will come with a higher price tag and deductible. It can be confusing and frustrating to deal with medical bills and insurance claims, so call your insurance provider for a detailed explanation of your coverage, benefits, and financial exposure (out-of-pocket costs).

Here is what insurance will typically cover as it relates to addiction:

- Detox and stabilization
- Psychiatric care
- Medications
- Residential treatment
- PHP and IOP

- Counseling services
- Drug testing and lab work

Here is what insurance will typically NOT cover:

- Licensed treatment centers using a religious exemption
- Unlicensed residential recovery centers
- Sober transportation
- Most sober living facilities
- Sober companion or escort
- Sober coaching

This is only a general summary. There are some situations that will deviate, and the insurance industry is also changing to keep pace with the constant evolution of the treatment industry. Any service or product that is not "clinical" by nature, or is not licensed, will usually not be covered by insurance.

Navigating the process of selecting a treatment facility and dealing with insurance providers can be challenging. It is helpful to begin this process with a solid understanding of the following terms:

- **Interventions** – I will go into detail about the planning and execution of interventions in Chapter Five. For this list, what is important is that you understand that although this is a professional service, it is not clinical or medical. It is often necessary to leverage someone into making better choices, but it is not something insurance typically covers.
- **Licensed Treatment Centers Using a Religious Exemption** – When applying for a license with the state, a provider can select a religious

exemption. This means the program is exempt from any and all regulations set forth by the state. It may be an exceptional program, but it will not be eligible for any accreditations, nor will it be recognized by the insurance industry. The provider is free to run the program as he sees fit, which can be good or bad. There is no rule against religious programs; you just need to understand the difference between a religious program that has a standard license or an exempt license if you plan on using insurance.

- **Unlicensed Residential Recovery Programs** – This model has become a popular and more affordable alternative to residential treatment. Much like the religious exemption, it is not eligible for accreditations or insurance coverage. These programs are often in the 90-day range, offering a 12-step immersion program at a reduced price. Typically, a 90-day program costs about the same as a 30-day program in a licensed residential treatment center. Before your child enters any unlicensed program, you need to do your homework so you know what you are paying for. Call to ask about the program and look for any reviews or references. Unlicensed does not necessarily mean unqualified. Many unlicensed programs are very reputable and effective.
- **Sober or Transitional Living Programs** – Since these programs vary in the level of proficiency, education, and structure, they cannot be quantified on any scale. Again, you must do your homework and look into any place you are considering. Look at the website, call with any questions, tour the facility, and ask for references. These programs can also provide

aftercare. They are affordable and important pieces of the whole recovery process; the addicted loved one learns to stand on his own two feet by working, paying bills, and cleaning up his past. Having the support and accountability that these programs provide is indispensable during the precarious stage of early recovery.

- **Sober Transportation** – This is a service that is often combined with interventions, or utilized when someone in early recovery needs to travel but still requires a high level of accountability. A responsible and sober individual escorts someone from one place to the next, either by car or plane. This might be to a treatment center, to appear in court, or to attend a meeting.

- **Sober Companion/Escort** – This is the hired professional who travels with or escorts someone in early recovery on important but hazardous trips and meetings. I have a friend with an office in Los Angeles and New York who does a phenomenal job providing this service. However, it does not come cheap; it is like having a sober bodyguard and chauffer rolled into one person.

- **Sober Coaching** – This involves hiring a person to help with various tasks, such as finding a job or a 12-step meeting. This position remains somewhat undefined, with services that overlap those provided by sober living programs. Typically, after a sober coach is hired, he offers an agreed upon number of visits or coaching sessions. The idea is to offer direction to someone who is early in recovery and who is not participating in any other form of aftercare.

You need to remember two important terms relating to insurance coverage:

1. **Medical Necessity** – A medical necessity must be documented at the time of admission, otherwise insurance claims will be denied.
2. **Meeting Criteria** – Much like medical necessity, criteria must be met and documented at the time of admission into any clinical program or service.

Consider this example: If someone suffering withdrawals is arrested and spends several days in the county jail, she no longer meets criteria for services. The withdrawals are gone. There is no longer a medical necessity to admit this person into a residential program. She obviously needs the help, but she must be currently using or experiencing withdrawals to meet criteria. Since no one wants her to use again, just to get help, there is a need to look at other available services. She could still meet criteria for aftercare, depending on what drugs she used and how much time has passed. A viable option could be a residential recovery program or structured sober living program.

Sometimes parents spend so much time weighing their options that they miss the boat to have insurance pay for the care. For example, when someone leaves residential treatment and goes to sober living, but decides to wait two weeks before enrolling into PHP or IOP for aftercare, he will likely NOT meet criteria. Here is the reasoning: The insurance company knows that the addicted loved one has been clean while in treatment, and it expected him to enroll into PHP or IOP immediately after entering a sober living program. If there is a delay of a few weeks, the insurance company believes that he must not need that level of care and will deny benefits.

Once your child has been approved for services, you must act right away or you will risk losing coverage. If you are checking with the insurance company prior to an intervention, let them know you are planning the intervention so they will know there must be some time before it is performed. A skilled interventionist will also be well versed in this process and can plan accordingly.

All this can make a very tedious and confusing time for the addicted loved one and the family. I believe that after reading the rest of the book you will be better equipped to handle everything that comes with the treatment and recovery process.

CHAPTER FOUR

THE LEGAL COMMUNITY

Has your child been arrested, or have you ever thought about calling the police on your child? Are you afraid that he will get arrested and throw away his future? Do you believe that your child would never get mixed up in anything that would result in criminal charges? If you can say yes to just one of these questions, this chapter contains essential information for you. You may have never needed to be familiar with the criminal justice system up to now, but for the sake of your child you must be aware of how it works.

We do our best to protect our children from bad influences. In fact, we usually take painstaking measures to prevent certain people and activities from ever coming close to them. But we never want to think that it may be our child who is the problem or the bad influence.

One night when I was a teenager still too young to drive, my friend David and I snuck out and rode our bicycles a few miles to a convenience store in Plano, Texas. We were playing pinball when a police officer walked in and asked us if our parents knew we were out. One of us looked at the cop and snapped, "Hey man, we just walked out the front door." The officer did not like our attitudes. Since we were out past curfew, he said he could either call our parents to come get us or take us to jail. At two o'clock in the morning, he called my house and woke up my parents. At first they thought the police officer must have been mistaken, but they checked my room and found pillows bunched up under the sheet to look like I was sleeping. Needless to say, they were very upset with me.

I remember my dad telling me that he had always blamed my friends for my actions, but now he realized that perhaps *I* was the bad influence. He said he was going to call the parents of my friends to tell them that I was the problem, and that they might consider keeping their kids away from me. Sounds harsh doesn't it? He never made the calls but his eyes were opened.

In this chapter I will help you find your way within the legal community and show you how to make it an ally in your fight to save your child. There are many myths and exaggerations about this community, and I want to help you understand what is real and what is not.

WHY DO WE NEED TO KNOW ABOUT THE LEGAL COMMUNITY?

If people use drugs long enough, they will most likely find their way into the legal system. If we understand the legal community as a whole, it will be much easier to maneuver when that day comes. Whether your child gets into legal trouble or not, you will not want to skip over this chapter. Knowledge of the legal system and how it works is one of the most powerful tools I have when it comes to performing interventions.

This is not a scare tactic; it saves many lives. It is what saved my life.

Most of us have heard that if we find ourselves or our children in legal trouble, we should hire the very best attorney and quickly make arrangements for posting bail. We immediately jump to the thought that a criminal record will ruin our child's chance at school or any hope of a meaningful career. This line of thinking is not necessarily wrong; however, I am going to challenge many of your beliefs about it.

It is true that a record, particularly a felony record, will greatly hamper your child's aspirations in certain fields. Banking, law enforcement, the military, and many residential service industries that require a license or bond (just to name a few), will no longer be viable career choices. A first offense may derail your child's chances of realizing her dreams of a certain career goal. In that instance, it may be wise to do all you can to beat the charge. The real question becomes what do you do once your child has had a second or third entanglement with the law? Do you continue to rush to her side and do your best to minimize the pending charges? At some point it won't really matter how much money you throw at a problem; the situation will be significant enough that it is completely out of your hands and you and your child will be at the mercy of the court.

RETHINKING OUR RESPONSES

Maybe it's not a bad idea to let him sit in the county jail for a while before facing the music in court for a DWI charge. In Texas, as with most states, the third DWI becomes a felony; there is no quick fix, no matter what you do. Perhaps if your child had had to suffer some significant consequences for his first charge, before the stakes were so high, he might have rethought his actions. Maybe, maybe not. But if he continues his behavior, you could end up bankrupt from legal fees, and your child would still end up in prison or worse. Eventually, the odds are great that someone is going to die, either your child or someone else's. If your adult child kills someone while driving under the influence, he could spend the rest of his life (and yours) incarcerated. Unfortunately, this happens with alarming frequency.

Sometimes parents believe that unless they protect their child from every hardship they are bad parents; it is ingrained in them to "fix" things and save their children at any cost. There is a term I want you to get familiar with: *prolonging their misery*. It's what happens when instincts to protect your young mean leaving sound reasoning behind. Sometimes in your efforts to be "good parents" you allow destructive and deadly behavior to continue. Your child is not learning the lesson; she believes that you will always be there to bail her out of whatever trouble she finds. The stakes are just too high to let this behavior continue.

One of the hardest things my father ever had to say to me took place when I called him from jail the second time. It was not my second time in jail, but it was the second time that I thought I needed his help to make everything go away. I remember calling and saying that I was in serious trouble and needed his help. In my mind he was going to come and bail me out of jail and supply me with the best lawyer money could buy. What he said was, "Son, I'm really sorry to hear that. You call us and let us know how everything works out when you get out of jail." No money and no help, just the sound of him hanging up the phone. I was stunned. Years later I realized how incredibly difficult this was for him. My father loved me enough to say no, enough to be uncomfortable and let me experience the fallout from my own actions.

In Chapter Nine, I will describe in greater detail how I was especially stubborn. I now believe that every minute of the consequences I endured prepared me to find and excel at my true calling: to help others recover.

UNDERSTANDING SOME LEGAL TERMS

Your knowledge of the legal system must include a solid understanding of several key legal terms. A **felony** is a serious criminal offense for which you can be fined up to $10,000 and be sentenced to a state penitentiary for a period of between six months and life. You also may lose your right to vote, possess a gun, or obtain certain state occupational licenses. Felonies include aggravated assault, burglary, and DWI, third offense. In Texas there are five categories of felonies.

FELONY	PENALTY
Capital	Death or life in prison without parole
First-degree	5 to 99 years in a state prison and/or a fine of not more than $10,000
Second-degree	2 to 20 years in a state prison and/or a fine of not more than $10,000
Third-degree	2 to 10 years in a state prison and/or a fine of not more than $10,000

State jail	180 days to 2 years in a state jail and/or a fine of not more than $10,000

A **misdemeanor** is a less serious criminal offense for which you can be fined $4,000 or less and be sentenced to county jail for up to one year. You do not lose any civil rights for a misdemeanor conviction. Misdemeanors include simple assault, theft, and DWI, first or second offense. This information is based on laws in Texas. Many states have the same or similar laws, but you will want to check the laws in your specific state.

There are three classes of misdemeanors: A, B, and C.

MISDEMEANOR	PENALTY
Class A	Not more than 1 year in a county jail and/or a fine of not more than $4,000
Class B	Not more than 180 days in a county jail and/or a fine of not more than $2,000
Class C	A fine of not more than $500

The penal code sets broad sentencing guidelines for each class and degree of criminal charge. Sentencing is generally left up to the judge. However, the judge may receive recommendations from the prosecutor and, in certain cases, from the jury. The judge has significant latitude to impose the sentence he believes is the most appropriate. He can also accept *or reject* a plea bargain.

The Texas Health and Safety Code sets the possession law, dividing controlled substances into five penalty groups, plus a marijuana category. While some of the substances are legal prescription drugs, it is illegal to possess them without a valid prescription. The Texas health code establishes the punishments for illegal possession. See pages 221–225 of Appendix II for a more detailed look at the penalties for drug use.

WHO IS A PART OF THE LEGAL COMMUNITY?

The following is a description of the people you would likely encounter in our legal system; each person can play a vital role in leveraging someone to make better decisions. Being armed with this information will help you understand how to use the legal community to help you.

The Arresting Officer

He or she may not seem to be the one who would offer help, but in my experience, these men and women make some of the very best interventionists. I spent many years believing they were all just out to get me. I even wrote a song while trying to make a career in music about how they ruined my life. Looking back, there were a number of officers who asked me if I had ever thought about getting clean or asking for help. Typically, I was just rude or silent, but it didn't stop them from asking. As I have developed relationships with our local police department, I have always been impressed by how many officers have really tried to connect the dots and get help for those who need it the most. Over the years, everyone from patrol officers and lieutenants, all the way up to the chief of police, has contacted me to meet with someone who needed help. As a result, my team and I have been given access to our jails to make contact and evaluate substance abuse issues with various inmates. This has become one of our strongest relationships.

The police see firsthand the destruction and devastation of addiction. The majority of the officers I have met want to see these men and women get well. When someone like me approaches law enforcement and offers available help with addiction, it is almost always a welcome conversation. They also understand that jail combined with the offer of help is a most effective tool.

A certain officer who had arrested me on more than one occasion once said, "I bet you think I arrest you every time I see you. People probably tell you that you are just paranoid when you complain about me arresting you every time I see you. Well, the truth is I do. I have identified you as a problem on my streets and I am going to remove the problem, so every time I see you out here at night, I am going to stop you. One of four things is going to happen. One, you will get help and stop being a problem. Two, you are going to get tired of me and move away. Three, I am going to catch you committing a serious offense. Four, you are going to die. Whichever happens, you will get off my streets, and until you figure that out I will be here to arrest you."

This officer didn't hate me; he was trying to get me to see that I needed help and he was not going to let me continue to put everyone else at risk. He played his part in helping me see my problems.

When you contact the police department, don't take the position that some rogue cop targeted your child. You can't just speak to someone in charge, asserting that it must be a misunderstanding, and expect him to release your child without charging her. My advice is to call the jail information line to find out exactly what the charges are and if bond has been set. Usually, nothing can be done until morning if the arrest was at night.

Almost all police departments have someone who can talk to you about your options. In Denton, Texas, we have a wonderful social worker who is there for the sole purpose of working with you. Whether the person committed an offense or is a victim, he is there to help. Once you have contacted this person, you can learn about resources or just receive advice on how to get your child back on track. You may be able to speak to the arresting officer and ask for his insight on the issue. Officers are not clinicians or social workers. They are, however, on the front line, and they see young men and women going down the wrong path every day. They may not know of any resources, but they do have experience with what will happen if certain behaviors continue.

You may not like what the arresting officer has to say about your child. *It is important that you listen with an open mind.* She will likely be delighted that you are seeking the truth so that you can take corrective measures. Not all police officers will be helpful, but most are. In the rare times that they aren't, you will need to refrain from becoming combative or demanding an apology; that is not going to benefit anyone. It's possible that one day you will be friends with the officer who held your child accountable and shined a light on her deadly behaviors.

In today's climate, law enforcement has taken a beating in the media. These men and women put their lives on the line to protect us and some have been accused of having malicious intentions. During the writing of this book, five police officers were killed and nine others were injured in Dallas. That is 14 innocent officers shot by a sniper, not to mention all the other attacks on law enforcement across the country. Despite all this, they are still here to help.

In the following chapters you will learn how law enforcement can aid you even if your child has never been arrested. Let me repeat: I find law enforcement to be the most effective tool at my disposal when performing an intervention.

The Lawyer

This is the professional who may hold the key to freedom, or at least reduced time in jail. There are many lawyers I know who will not take on a case unless the person in question is willing to get help. The conventional attitude used to be that if you sent your client to treatment, you were admitting to guilt, but things have changed. It is better to attack the problem head on, which may mean treatment of some kind. Many lawyers are well informed about these matters.

It is hard to say which relationship is most important, but this is certainly a crucial one. Collaborating effectively with an attorney makes for great outcomes. From the initial jail visit to the courtroom, a good attorney recognizes the benefit of having a treatment provider or interventionist in her corner. I cannot tell you how many people have been released into my organization's custody while awaiting court because of this vital relationship. The attorney wants the very best outcome for her client, and she often has a number of contacts and resources to accomplish that goal. I have witnessed miracles in the courtroom when we worked together for a better outcome.

It is important for everyone to stay in his lane. The attorney is the professional expert regarding legal matters, which means you *must* follow his lead. This professional will tell you exactly how to conduct yourself in and out of the courtroom. When first meeting with the attorney, make your desires, expertise, willingness, and availability for court known, but beyond that, you need to take the back seat and follow his professional directions.

A Good Example
An attorney I know called me to meet him at the county jail to interview someone. Together, we went to the jail and laid out a plan for his client. I introduced myself and explained what I do and how I could help. A few weeks later we were all in court together, where I was called to the stand and asked a series of questions by both the defense and the prosecution. Since we had met ahead of time, I explained to the court that I was willing to help the client and had space for him in my program. The defense attorney asked questions to highlight certain aspects of our facility and program. When the prosecutor questioned me I was prepared and answered his questions satisfactorily. The end result was that the young man was released to my custody and entered into our program. Several months later we were all in court again, and the disposition of his case was favorable because he had been offered help and took advantage of it. Without this collaboration, the young man would have sat in jail for several months waiting for his date in court. Chances are that without his ability to receive help and demonstrate that he was serious, the outcome would have been far less favorable.

A Bad Example

A woman in a neighboring city wrote me from jail and asked me to contact her attorney about helping in her case. When the attorney called me back he mentioned that I was the expert they needed for court, that he had heard great things, and expected a great outcome. I told him that I had no prior knowledge of his client, and that we should all meet at least a week or two before court. He assured me that would happen, but with each passing day he put me off; he said we would have plenty of time to meet before court. On the day of his client's court appearance, he was late and we had less than five minutes to talk. Clearly, he was not interested in going over suitable questions. I wanted to walk away, but I had told this woman that I would try to help her.

Once we were in court, it quickly became obvious that he had no real idea who I was or what I did. He addressed me as "Dr. Wisenbaker" and asked me how long I had been a doctor. I am not a doctor. Flustered, he then referred to my program as something it was not, and again I had to correct him. By this point I was aggravated but maintained my composure for court. In my mind I wanted to say, "I think what you wanted to ask me was...," but in court you can only answer the questions you are asked. If the lawyer had made the effort to meet with me in advance, this would have gone in a completely different direction.

As the prosecutor started, it was also obvious that he knew exactly which services we performed and which services we did not. Knowing that his opponent had made claims that were inaccurate, he immediately pointed out the inconsistencies. He suggested that since I was not a doctor, the court was misled and could not agree to the request made to allow the defendant into our program. Since the defense attorney failed to ask the questions that would have made us look like the right choice, the prosecutor was certainly not about to.

The judge, realizing the unprepared state of the defense, asked me to explain exactly who I was and what I did. By the time it was all said and done, the judge considered the request. However, the defendant was so shaken by how bad everything was going in the courtroom, that she decided to take the prosecution's offer of seven months in jail followed by nine months of SAFP (Substance Abuse Felony Punishment). This was not the desired outcome, and it might have been completely avoided. This was by far the least prepared attorney that I have come across, and he was angry with me for his lack of knowledge and preparedness. Based on some of the comments he made in court, it appeared that this particular lawyer knew very little about addiction, while the prosecution and judge seemed informed and knowledgeable.

One of the reasons that most lawyers offer a free initial consultation is so they can learn the facts of the case, and you can ask questions to determine whether or not they are the right lawyer for you. Use this time wisely. If your attorney seems too busy, or is unwilling to answer questions and look into available resources, you need to find another attorney. It is also wise to talk with more than one attorney, in the same way you would get a second opinion from a doctor. One of my friends who has a private practice in our city requires prospective clients to speak to another attorney before paying him a retainer fee. Not all lawyers are this ethical but many are. When referring someone to a lawyer, I always refer to someone who will do what is best for the client regarding his addiction.

When hiring a lawyer, you need to discuss your intentions and desired outcomes. Let her know that you are open to her recommendations for help. If you have already selected a program, tell her what you are thinking; her insight on these matters should not be taken lightly. Not every lawyer has a detailed list of available programs but many do. If you have researched a number of programs, you should be willing to share your findings with the attorney because this information will help her with the next family in need.

Once you have hired an attorney, he is working for your child and cannot share any information with you without your child's permission. As odd as this sounds, especially if you are paying the fees, this is for everyone's protection. You need to understand this and not be angry with the attorney, as he must abide by the law with respect to privacy. For this reason, you will want to be very clear about your intentions before paying the fees.

A lawyer is your lifeline if you are honest with him; encourage your child to be straightforward and honest. Tell her that the lawyer is not allowed to tell you what she says. This may seem counterproductive, but knowing every little detail is not necessary. Your child has been caught, and now you are doing everything in your power to help; that is what is important. Knowing the specifics won't help you, and actually may be more truth than you can handle.

The Prosecutor/District Attorney

We have mentioned the prosecutor several times. How

can he be helpful when his job is to find someone guilty? At first I had that same question, but several of my experiences have answered it for me. After a few people had been released into my custody, the District Attorney's office looked into who I was and what kind of program I offered. Upon close examination of our theories and policies, many members of the DA's office began to support our work, knowing that the individual would be held accountable.

It is our level of understanding, structure, and accountability that often makes our program attractive to the prosecution. The job of the DA's office is to hold people accountable, which is primarily done through convictions. They need a win just as much as the defense, which means that both sides are often willing to negotiate. One of my friends joked to me that, "You know it's a good settlement when both parties leave unhappy." The idea here is that a settlement or deal is a give-and-take negotiation. No jail time with probation is still a win for both sides in many cases; the defense managed no jail time, and the prosecution managed to get a conviction.

While you need to understand the mindset and goals of the prosecution, you don't talk with them or ask for any advice unless *you* are pressing charges against your child. (In some cases, you may find yourself pressing charges against your child to ensure the safety of your home and your other children.) Outside of that situation, do not talk to the prosecution without consulting your attorney. Remember that their job is to find your child guilty. You may think you are helping by explaining the circumstances surrounding your child's charges, but you actually may be making their case. Your attorney will direct you on what to say if you are contacted by the

DA's office. If they contact you, simply say you must first contact your attorney.

The Judge

The last thing you want to do is come to court unprepared, talk back, dress poorly, or lie to the judge. This goes for everyone and not just the client. There are things you need to know about almost any judge. First, judges are human. Second, they want to be fair and compassionate. Third, they are responsible for holding people accountable.

Human? You bet. If you become offensive or try to make a mockery out of their courtroom, you will be held accountable.

Compassionate, because in most cases, the judge wants to give the offender the ability to improve her life, even when mandatory jail time is required. If a deal has been reached by the prosecution and defense, the judge must also approve it. If part of the deal requires the client to enter into a treatment program the judge is familiar with, he is likely to approve the deal. On the other hand, if the deal is viewed as too soft or more like a vacation, chances are he will object to it.

I have spent a lot of time in the courthouse and I have been in front of each judge in our county. Many of our current judges are familiar with our program and consider it a viable option in many cases. They also have an understanding of what consequences can be expected if the client is not serious or willing to comply with a treatment plan. This is important to them because of their responsibility to hold people accountable. Judges want to be reelected!

In my opinion, the best time to enter into a program like ours is prior to the actual trial date, so that the prosecution and the judge can see how the defendant progresses. This allows the defendant a real opportunity to make positive changes before a final judgment is rendered. Each party can move forward in court without hesitation, one way or the other.

If the defense has done a good job of presenting the nature of the program, it becomes obvious to everyone that the burden of action is placed on the client alone. If the client does well and makes positive changes, recidivism rates are improved and the court looks as though it has used good judgment.

If the client is combative and unwilling to change on any level, the request for help appears to be nothing more than a song and dance to avoid jail. In such a case, the client will ultimately fail to comply with a structured program and will be returned to the court, at which time the judge will impose a definite and appropriate sentence.

The court understands that a good program only works if the client is willing to participate and takes the opportunity seriously. The court does not have to offer such opportunities. As stated earlier, judges want to be compassionate and help people, but sometimes a client is released to me and sometimes the motion is denied. The judge is not angry with me, nor angry with the defense. This usually happens when the judge has already extended opportunities or released the client prior to the trial, and she did not comply with the terms of her release. Rather than allowing someone like this back into the community, it is sometimes safer for all concerned to keep her in the jail until the case is resolved.

Sometimes, and my lawyer friends hate when I say this, jail is exactly what is needed. Consequences can be powerful motivators to make positive changes. Many lawyers would like to believe that just their pep talk and a good deal in court is enough to make the difference; we all want to believe that it was our part in the equation that effected a change. I would say it is the collaboration of all involved that makes an opportunity both attractive and possible. But at the end of the day, it is the *client alone* who either accepts the help or does not.

I love being a part of this system because many times we are the only help available to someone, and without our participation the cycle of addiction would continue. We can look back and see that many individuals have benefitted from our collaborations with the legal community. Everyone involved gets the opportunity to see great outcomes where lives are saved, families are reconnected, and children have a stable, healthy, and loving environment. These results are very gratifying; they reenergize us to continue our collaborations.

Many of my team members are living examples of these partnerships. All members of the court are impressed every time one of them makes an appearance on behalf of a client. There is almost nothing sweeter in our world than a previous defendant standing up in the very same court, testifying on behalf of another as an expert in our field.

To conclude this discussion about our legal system, I will say that I am a big fan. This is often the first time someone is held accountable where the family cannot swoop in and fix everything. It can be the very thing that saves someone's life. Some of you might think that this is overreaching and melodramatic. If so, I encourage you to go to your computer and Google stats for teenage overdose deaths in your state. Then look up all drug and alcohol driving deaths including vehicle accidents. The numbers are staggering and real, no matter where you live.

There is no guarantee that someone will not re-offend, even if he is allowed to sit in the county jail and face his charges. Some of us are especially stubborn and act foolishly for longer periods of time.

In my own life, I always knew I would have to face any new charges without my family paying my fines or hiring the best lawyer available. I knew the State of Texas was more powerful than I, and I knew that eventually the state would lock me up for life if I continued to behave as I did. Even though it was my career in music that made me question my actions, it was the State of Texas and a wise judge who brought me to my knees and offered me the ability to get help when I finally asked for it. A career made me want it, jail made me willing, and the court allowed me the opportunity. This is why I encourage you to understand, value, and cultivate these relationships with members of the legal system.

CHAPTER FIVE

THE INTERVENTION

Let's say you have confronted your child and set boundaries he would not keep. Perhaps he's willing to go to a 12-step meeting or even treatment if necessary. Fantastic. But what if he isn't? What if he isn't willing to do anything? What if he continues to disregard your boundaries and gets belligerent and further out of control? He becomes more distant and you have a stranger in your midst. This is where some difficult decisions need to be made. Each family will have different needs; they may require different tactics, levels of care, or have different financial resources.

As a family member, this may be the most significant and difficult chapter to read. The family has the most power to help or hurt the addicted loved one's chances of recovery, but family members usually need some direction and support to be effective.

This is why most families find it best to hire a professional interventionist. The questions, conversations, and directions featured in this chapter are almost always taken more seriously from someone outside the family who is experienced in such matters. Going it alone risks decisions made from emotions and tension, blame, and finger pointing. It is impossible to be detached and objective when a loved one's life is on the line. Also, it is very difficult to get everyone on the same page, and in order to have a successful intervention, it is crucial that it start there.

There are many different styles and models for performing interventions. There are no required certifications as this is a non-clinical service that relies heavily on instincts, experience, and knowledge. Nevertheless, training and education are valuable, and standards in the industry are constantly evolving. In my opinion, some of the very best interventionists are in recovery themselves; it is the combination of their training and experience that makes them valuable and effective.

Each intervention and family are different, and each one calls for different techniques. This is where sharp instincts are required. One size does not fit all, and a good interventionist will determine the best approach after conducting interviews and getting a clear sense of the addict's and the family's history.

When selecting an interventionist, ask about experience and ask for references. This is, by nature, a very personal and private family matter. I find that many families are so grateful for the help, they are willing to write a letter of reference or even talk to a family who is considering the process.

PRE-INTERVENTION AND THE FAMILY

Every time we prepare for an intervention and sit down with the family, we are on a fact-finding mission. Often, one or more family members have their own ideas about how this should look and how I should behave, but I start off the very same way I started this book. After quick introductions and opening pleasantries, I immediately acknowledge the elephant in the room: that we are all there because they are afraid that their child/sibling /parent/friend is going to die. I follow with, "Knowing what drugs she is doing, if nothing is done, the odds are greatly increased that the very phone call you fear the most is the one you are going to get." I let them know that I cannot guarantee that I can change that outcome, *no one can.* But I assure them that their willingness to even consider this process indicates their commitment to change and offers an opportunity to greatly reduce the chances that the dreaded phone call ever comes. And what I can guarantee is that the family can find peace in the middle of this storm, whether or not their loved one recovers, if they follow my direction. Interventions aren't only for the addict.

Typically, at this point I have their undivided attention. I then start my fact-finding mission. How old is this person? Where does she live, who does she live with, and who pays the rent? Does she have a job, what does she do, and has she been in trouble at work due to her addiction? Does she have a car and, if so, who is paying for gas, maintenance, car payments, registration, and insurance? Is she in a relationship and, if so, is her partner willing to help or is he part of the problem? Are there children and, if so, where do they live? Who is paying child support? What does she do for entertainment and who pays for that?

I ask all of these questions and many more. What I almost always find out is that someone in the family is financing some part of her life. This person believes that he is helping, but what I need him to see is that an active life of addiction is never sustainable. When people help with car payments, insurance, rent, or even groceries, they are actually facilitating the addict's lifestyle.

This is where I always meet resistance and this is where you must take a very hard look at your own situation.

The typical American family of five with an addicted child almost always looks like this: Mom and dad are at odds and possibly headed for divorce court, if it hasn't already happened. The addicted child thinks everything is a joke or plays the victim, and the other two siblings are angry with everyone. The family is in fact fractured, and the other two siblings are left to watch the family unit go bankrupt and dissolve in front of their very eyes. They are left out and disgusted that every family discussion or gathering revolves around the addicted sibling. If the family continues down this path, it will eventually become fragmented and possibly never again operate as a healthy unit. Everyone becomes bitter and isolated. To top everything off, when the inevitable tragedy takes place, they are unable to comfort each other.

This is not an absolute. However, when the family will not change, this is what I have seen happen over and over. Without change there will only be misery.

If the addicted loved one is allowed to lose the car, job, home, or another significant item, it might be what is needed for him to see that he cannot continue. When you say no, he will beg, cry, and call you horrible things to get his way. If you stand firm, his lifestyle will crumble and he will be faced with the fact that he is in real trouble. This period of time can last minutes, hours, weeks, or even years, but chances are eventually he will ask for the kind of help he really needs—help with his addiction.

Either way, the remaining members of the family can start healing once they are united and have stopped contributing to the downfall of a child. This may take counseling and it will not happen overnight, but the family can be healed.

Be careful that once your child asks for help, you don't reinstate all of the financial aid you used to provide. She has a long road ahead of her, but there are many things she must do on her own. Eventually, there will be times that you can help in an appropriate manner, but that will not be the day she walks out of treatment. If after treatment everything goes back to the way it was, everything will go back to the way it was, *including the addiction.* Your financial aid should be used on treatment services and continuing aftercare.

RESPONDING TO COMMON EXCUSES

In this section, I show how I typically respond to each of the common excuses the family might give me. Remember that we are preparing for an intervention to save a life, so jobs and cars are not a concern of mine, and they should not be a concern of yours. What's more important, his life or his job?

1. He has to have a car so he can keep his job.

Reply: He doesn't need a car if he can't pay for it with his *own* money. Maybe if he is in danger of losing his job, he will take the request to go to treatment more seriously.

    2. I'm afraid that if we take anything away from him he will go into a tailspin.

Reply: A tailspin is exactly what we need if he refuses treatment. We are not writing him off; we are just showing that we are willing to let him be uncomfortable so that he will become willing to accept our help. Your resolve must be stronger than his. We are pushing everything to a head while staying in front of him and offering the help he needs.

    3. I'm doing it for their kids.

Reply: A temporary order for you or another family member to take custody of the children is what's best for everyone. I have seen parents suddenly take recovery seriously when they lose custody of their kids. If they're using, they aren't in a good place to be raising children.

    4. We're good parents and we're helping our child.

Reply: No one is questioning your parenting skills or your love for your child, but you have to admit that you are in over your head. This is where I can help because this is where my expertise is. If it were any other medical issue, you would take him to the doctor and not second-guess the doctor's directions. Think of me as your addiction specialist, and just like any other ailment there is a long road to recovery where you must follow directions.

5. If I don't do what he wants, he will take matters into his own hands. He could end up in jail or worse.

Reply: This is often just a threat to get what he wants, but jail could be the best thing that could happen. When I find out that someone has legal issues, including probation or being out of jail on a bail bond, I immediately use it as leverage. If he refuses treatment, I direct the person who is holding the bond to cancel it with the bail bondsman. This way I let him know that the choice is to get in my truck and go to treatment (where it is nice, has professionals who want to help, and has good food), or he can get in the police truck and return to jail. There he will sit for months awaiting trial and then be viewed as someone who had an opportunity for help but refused it. If he is on probation, I let him know that I will contact his probation officer and report that he is using and refusing our help.

6. If I don't give it to him, he will just steal it.

Reply: If he steals, call the police. Again, contrary to what you might believe, he is safer in jail than on the street. A few weeks or months in jail and his entire outlook may change.

7. His lifestyle is so dysfunctional that he can't be satisfied with it; he just needs time and direction to find his way.

Reply: As I stated before, his lifestyle is working for him on some level.

8. If he can't make his payments to the

court/probation/child support, he will go to jail.

Reply: Jail is a consequence he cannot just explain away. Given a little time in jail, he might accept help. If you are going to bail him out, make sure he goes from jail directly to treatment. Do not let him stop for anything. You can always have the attorney stipulate that treatment and aftercare are a condition of his bond. If you do not have everything lined up when he is released, you have already lost again. He must be transported directly from point A to point B.

9. I'm afraid if I don't help, he will die.

Reply: It's all about the right help, and once we stop helping him kill himself, the odds are increased that he will be okay.

I don't know how I can be any clearer: If you give in, you are financing the addiction, prolonging his misery, and almost certainly contributing to his death. I'm sorry if that sounds blunt and rude, but this is life and death, and the sooner you are able to see that, the sooner you can start actually helping him.

Now I want you to think about the following two example of real people and real situations.

Example 1
There is a woman I once worked with who actually pulled her own money out of the bank and regularly drove into Dallas to buy heroin for her son.

How could this happen? It was easier than you think. The young man would tell his mother that if she didn't help him, he would have to go out and do something really bad to get his drugs. So bad that he might be killed in the process or arrested and locked up for 25 or more years.

The first few times he mentioned such a ridiculous request, she was enraged and they fought until he disappeared for days at a time. Each time he returned home, she let him in and provided medical attention and food. She was just thankful that he was alive and made it home safely. This went on for some time, and she reluctantly handed her son money on a number of occasions, knowing that he could die or be placed under arrest. In an attempt to keep him safe and out of jail, she took him to the place he purchased his drugs and then returned home where—in her mind—he was safe.

Her son, who was 27, had previous drug charges that drained much of her savings and ultimately resulted in her divorce. If arrested again for felony drug charges, he would surely go to prison for a long time. She was so frightened about losing her son to the legal system that she started making regular trips to Dallas *by herself* to buy her son's heroin. When I asked her about this, she broke down and said, "If I don't do this for him, something really bad will happen. I know it's wrong, but I have no choice. At least I know where he is."

This single mother, who was getting further and further into debt, is also a licensed nurse—someone who knows firsthand the dangers of drug overdoses and the long-term health effects. She, of all people, knew better. If she were to be charged with a drug offense, she would forever lose her license. There is also the very real possibility that she could be robbed, sexually assaulted, or killed while attempting to purchase drugs. These possible consequences didn't occur to her son as he complained about how long it would take her, how little she bought, or the quality of the drugs. And it wouldn't have mattered if they had; he was so self-absorbed and imprisoned in his own addiction that he couldn't think of anyone other than himself and getting what he wanted.

This may sound extreme, and it is, but I have met three different women who did the exact same thing for similar reasons.

Example 2

I have a friend in the industry who was trying to work with a woman who was allowing her adult son to use drugs in her home. She insisted she had to continue doing so for the safety of her son. All of the pleading and education my friend offered fell on deaf ears, and within weeks her son died in his own bed from a heroin overdose. At the funeral, she told my friend that she was grateful that he passed in his own bed and not somewhere alone in a ditch.

My friend said she was sorry for her loss. Inside she was screaming, but she knew that no good would come from a lecture. The truth is that this woman inadvertently contributed to her own son's death. There is no guarantee that he would not have died anyway, but she could have greatly increased the odds of his survival by drawing a line in the sand and refusing to contribute to his drug usage. She simply could not see that she was prolonging his misery by making his lifestyle possible. In this case, I would say that jail would have been a great alternative because he would still be alive today.

Both of these women had it in their hearts to be helpful to their children, but they were not. That instinct that sends us, without hesitation, to snatch up a small child who is headed toward a busy road, is not the appropriate motivation when dealing with grown children.

Your job at this point is to take a very honest look at the family's role. Which family members are making the behavior possible, and how can you make them see the destructive nature of their actions? Sometimes there are those who cannot or will not stop, despite any conversation or enlightenment. They have become so engrossed in the daily actions of the afflicted loved one that they have ceased to have sound reasoning. Much like the addict's behavior, it has happened over time and has been dismissed as benign action based on love; individuals who suffer from this denial are often completely unwilling or unable to see it. Sometimes, relationships and emotions can make this impossible to navigate without the guidance of a trained interventionist. Understand that without help these persons will never change; they need treatment as much as the addict or alcoholic.

Parents can become offended and angry at the idea that they play a part in the addictive behaviors of their own family. They yell, "He is the problem, not me!! We are a good family in a good neighborhood with good friends!" I have witnessed grown men and women throw temper tantrums when such an idea is expressed. But now you need to put away completely the need to be right or place blame. At this point, *none of that matters*. This is life or death for someone, and you need to act accordingly. There is no time for anything other than taking corrective measures to save your family. You are under attack and you must win.

CONSEQUENCES OF OUR ACTIONS

This section presents a summary of some of the undesired and unintended consequences our own actions can have.

1. **The obvious enabling and funding of the addictive behaviors**

   As shown in the previous examples, this must stop or else the phone call you fear the most will likely become your reality.

2. **Contributing to the death of the family member they are trying to save**

   When this happens, the family will never be the same. The finger pointing, name-calling, and blame that follow can destroy the remainder of the family. Without professional help, the guilt alone can become overwhelming.

3. **Fractured relationships with various family members, including other children**

   Often we see the un-addicted, or "good" children, shuffled to the side as they become more resentful with each passing day. They are not just resentful toward their sibling; they are often even more so with the parent who is consumed with their addicted sibling. These children have been ignored or upstaged by bad behaviors—the very bad behaviors they were taught to avoid. They have lost their childhood to the family crisis of addiction, even though they have done nothing wrong. The family is fractured, vacations and happy holidays no longer exist, funds for school tuition are spent on treatment, and a burning resentment slowly turns into hatred. The ignored siblings often engage in their own risky behavior as a means to gain attention. They frequently have difficulties trusting others, leading to relationship problems of their own.

4. **Divorce**

    As the preceding outcomes indicate, all relationships are pushed to the brink. Spouses typically have different ideas about how the addicted family member should be treated, which leads to disagreements. It is just a matter of time before comments like, "You never really loved him," are thrown back and forth. Without help, divorce often becomes inevitable.

5. **Stress and anxiety**

    Life is stressful enough without addiction infiltrating your family. Trying to manage the life of the addict without taking corrective measures will lead to a high level of stress and anxiety. In turn, this brings about a whole new set of physical ailments, some of which can be deadly.

6. **Complete loss of self-worth**

    What happens when the addicted child gets well? If your entire life has revolved around one child's need for protection and care, where do you think you will be when she suddenly doesn't need it anymore? I can tell you where many end up. Having isolated themselves from the rest of the family, they are left completely alone and bitter. The recovered child can never make it up to the parent who gave up so much for her. The parent tells the child that she is ungrateful, and sometimes even suggests that she was better while using. Let that last statement sink in for a minute!

Do you see how we can get so far away from where we started that we might actually say something along those lines? We might as well say, "I wish you were dead," or "I wish I had just let you die that one night you were overdosing." Some of you reading this cannot imagine ever saying something so incomprehensible, and some of you have said these very statements. Addiction doesn't just take the addicted child to hell; it takes the entire family. If the child were to return to old behaviors, the family member in question would again feel a sense of purpose. Can you see why this person may also need treatment?

7. **Suicide**

Yes, suicide. If even half of the items listed above become one's reality, he might consider suicide as a viable option. It's not something that is given much thought or planning; it is something that becomes a possibility when we get to a place where we feel as though we cannot recover from our present situation and cannot bear to continue. It is more about stopping the pain.

Remember that family members have more to do with outcomes than anyone else. When they can't stop making misguided decisions, they need treatment just as urgently as the addicted member. If treatment is not sought, the cycle will continue; but there is help available for this level of codependency. Codependency is a word which I have avoided until now. If I had started the chapter with the term codependency, those who need to read this the most would skip right past it or set down the book altogether. It is a term we had to work up to, but make no mistake about it: This is codependency and it is just as destructive as any other addiction.

There are great programs available just for this situation. If you are the one who needs help in this area, you must accept it. You may find all of the support and change you need in Al-Anon, but you must be willing to do the work. If not, you must seek help elsewhere for the sake of your family as well as for yourself. If you need help selecting the appropriate treatment center for codependency, please email us at info@sontx.org. I have included a list of several community based resources at the end of the book. See pages 227 of Appendix IV.

WHAT IS AN INTERVENTION?

Strap in. It is time to make our stand and do our best to leverage our addicted loved one into making better choices. This process may only take minutes or it may last days or weeks. Be strong. Be prepared. Listen to your interventionist.

in·ter·ven·tion
in(t)ər'ven(t)SH(ə)n/
> Noun: intervention; Plural noun: interventions
> > *the action or process of intervening.*

1. action taken to improve a situation, especially a medical disorder.

2. an occasion in which a person with an addiction or other behavioral problems is confronted by a group of friends, family members, or other individuals in an attempt to persuade him to address the issue.

3. the act of inserting one thing between others.

In other words, an intervention is leveraging someone to make a better decision.

WHAT ABOUT WAITING FOR SOMEONE TO HIT BOTTOM?

This is one way you can go about it; wait until the day your child has lost enough and felt enough pain to question her own actions. It is effective, and many feel we should always go this route. Sadly, though, that day may never come, or it may come too late. It is long and it is painful for everyone. I'm not a fan of this school of thought. Do you have the stomach to watch your child suffer for years to come? To watch her accumulate so much legal trouble that she will never be able to live in a decent apartment complex or have a meaningful career, and possibly spend large chunks of her life wasting away in jail and prison?

Why do I have to wait to help my kid? The answer is, you don't. In fact, that is why I wrote this book. Do you have any idea how many people have died looking for their "bottom"? How many addicts have experienced years of suffering followed by everyone saying, "When you have had enough I guess you will get well"? That kind of sounds like, "If you were more important, I would try to help you." I know that many have been told that this is the only way someone could get well. I just need you to understand that it is not necessarily true.

This is the heart of an intervention: changing circumstances and finding a way to increase someone's willingness to accept help. When I am hired to perform an intervention, it is my job to raise the stakes and push everything to a head, forcing the hand of the addicted loved one. When it comes right down to saving someone's life, there are no hard and fast rules. How could there be? The addiction is taking *everything* from you and your family, so why would you hang back and wait for someone to achieve self-realization? Remember that the first system in our brain to be affected is the higher learning or decision-making system. If sound reasoning is the first thing to go, how reasonable is it to wait for someone without sound reasoning to decide it's time to make a sound decision?

THE COMPONENTS OF THE INTERVENTION

Once I speak to each family member and determine how best to proceed, I set a plan in motion. There are often some family members who continue enabling the very person we are trying to get into treatment. Those family members or friends are excluded from the actual intervention, as their lack of cooperation can derail this process in minutes. In many cases, I meet with the addicted loved one apart from the family, after our pre-intervention meeting, and perform the entire intervention without the family present. Again, every situation is different and sometimes we need the family members present. This decision is based on the interventionist's instincts.

Here are the main components of a successful intervention:

1. **Consultation/Pre-Intervention Meeting**

    This is the initial appointment where you meet with your interventionist. The situation is evaluated and if everyone decides to move forward, they sign agreements and develop a plan of action. If you have questions about your interventionist, this is the time to ask because once the agreement is signed and the interventionist is hired, you must follow his directions and let him do his job. If not, the interventionist may walk away from the table. If you are not willing to listen to him, don't hire him, but make sure you have a plan to meet with another interventionist. Interventionists spend a lot of time developing and executing a plan of action, so if you change your mind during the process they may rightfully keep the fees you have already paid.

2. **Plan of Action**

    You must know what the plan is. Where will she go? How will she get there? This should be finalized after the very first consultation. It is a time-consuming and research-heavy process that requires full disclosure of all relevant information. Having a well-versed, experienced interventionist with credible connections in the treatment field is priceless. Nothing can sidetrack an intervention faster than having the addicted loved one accept help and then there be none immediately available. Once the intervention is successful, she must go directly to treatment without stop or delay. Flights or vehicles have to be at the ready, a bed must already be secured, and bags must be packed. If no arrangements have been made, you risk having no available bed space at the desired center or having "sticker shock" when you hear the quoted out-of-pocket expenses. Even worse, your addicted loved one may change her mind in the chaos of gathering belongings, finding a center, researching benefits, waiting on travel arrangements, or even seeing the look on her father's face when quoted a price. There is nothing more harmful to a positive outcome than the addicted loved one perceiving that she is not worth the cost of rehab. This all must be handled beforehand.

Part of a great plan is planning for a variety of outcomes, such as the addicted loved one running out the door or wanting to start a physical altercation. Remember that for many of us, treatment is a very scary thing. When backed into a corner, animal instincts suggest fight or flight.

Without a solid, agreed upon plan of action, I will not participate and I suggest the family find a different interventionist (although I don't personally know of any interventionist who would go forward in that situation). It is bad for business and it is bad for the family. We also know when to walk away and let the family decide if they are ready and willing to work with us.

Experienced interventionists all have extensive networks of available detox hospitals, treatment centers, recovery centers, PHPs, IOPs, sober living facilities, and clinicians. These are people we know, have done business with, and trust. A great network of contacts makes our job easier. It is our job to help you put together the very best plan of action to fit your individual needs and resources.

3. **Agreement/Contract with Interventionist**

Each interventionist has his own contract and pricing structure. The base rate of an intervention may range anywhere from $3,000 to well over $50,000 as the length of contact and number of services covered vary. This price does not include additional costs, such as counseling, time spent locating the addicted loved one, or travel. The task at hand is to get the addicted loved one to make a better decision, period.

In any case, an agreement or contract must be signed after the initial consultation if there is going to be any further time or work invested in the intervention. Remember that there are no guarantees that the process will be successful, just as there are no guarantees that the addicted loved one will remain clean and sober after treatment. Much of the success depends on the actions of the family before and after the intervention. The following chapter will explain in great detail how the family can best support the addict's recovery efforts.

Most interventionists draft contracts that outline additional expenses, such as time beyond the typical intervention, hiring a private investigator when the addicted loved one has gone missing, additional counseling or treatment for other family members, case management terms, and transportation. As with any other contract, the more the terms are defined, the smoother the transaction will be.

Think about this in terms of retaining a lawyer: Every email, call, or meeting beyond an agreed amount has a charge. Most interventionists allow a considerable amount of time to invest in your family; however, multiple phone calls from multiple family members coming in at all hours of the night suggests that there may be some codependency issues that should be addressed. We want to answer your questions and do our best to put you at ease, but there is a limit to the time we have before additional charges may apply. My organization includes three months of case management to follow the addicted loved one during and after treatment to ensure aftercare is provided. We also include two additional family meetings throughout the treatment and aftercare phases. These are in addition to the initial consultation/family meeting, totaling three family sessions when appropriate.

Wherever you are and whoever you hire, the terms of the contract must be agreed upon and fulfilled before any additional work is performed.

4. Funding

Finding the funds is a huge factor, and sometimes a barrier, when trying to access treatment services. It is our job to find out what resources and/or insurance benefits are available and help you create a plan you can afford. It may not be what you envisioned. No one sets up a rehab fund for his child; instead, you plan for education, travel, automobiles, and weddings. No one wants to spend money on treatment or bail.

You need to look at treatment as lifesaving so that you can share all of those other milestones with your child. It may mean the education fund is utilized for treatment in hopes that one day your child will actually be able to attend college. It is my job to help you find realistic options, but you are going to have to spend some money and it must be secured prior to the intervention.

There are many alternative options to keep the price down. The last thing you want to do is spend every dime for an exotic treatment center and have nothing left for sober living and aftercare. Remember that this is like going into the hospital for a lifesaving procedure and then not following the directions of the doctor or going to follow-up appointments. Do that and you run the risk of undoing all the good that has been accomplished. We do not ignore aftercare when someone has cancer, just because it may come back anyway. We do as we are told and change our lifestyle so that we have the very best chance of success.

5. **Leverage**

Using leverage is the key to every intervention. Without it, the addicted loved one may see no reason to change. This is one of the very first things I identify when I plan an intervention. It may be a car, a place to live, a job, a relationship, financial resources, child custody, standing in the community, or in some instances, his freedom. Nothing is off limits here. If you find this particularly troubling, ask yourself, "Is [fill in the blank] more important than my child's life?"

My job is to quickly find the leverage and exploit it. If your child has been arrested and you posted bond, I can use this to persuade him to willingly go with me to treatment; I will let him know that if he refuses, we will revoke the bond and he will sit in jail for months awaiting trial. If his job is on the line and the employer is willing, I will make treatment a condition of keeping his job. If the employer does not know, I can use that as well. If his lifestyle is supplemented by the family, we will cut it off unless he leaves at once for treatment. If he is on probation . . .

you get the idea. Nothing is off limits.

If the addicted loved one refuses help and then contacts the family to beg, you are each instructed to ask if he is ready to accept help. If he is ready, give him the interventionist's phone number. If not, simply tell him that you cannot help, and you are not going to contribute to his death. Then hang up the phone. Every time.

6. **Contact with the Addicted Loved One**

During the initial contact, I make myself known and let her know that I am here to take her to treatment. When she refuses, I let her know that life as she knows it is about to change. Then I reveal my leverage. I hand her a card with my private cell number and tell her that it's okay if she loses it because her entire family has my number. If it is a bond issue, I let her know that she can either get into my car or the police car. If she starts making excuses, I repeat, "My car or the police car. You have five minutes." This way, she can be as mad at me as she wants; it will take the focus and anger off of the family to some extent. I can talk to her on the way to treatment, which may be a few hours. I have never had someone get out of the car at treatment still mad at me; one of our duties is to prepare her for treatment and get her to understand that this is for the best. It is not a quick conversation, but remember, we have a few hours together in the car or on a flight. Unlike a family member, no amount of pleading will change my resolve to complete the intervention and deliver her safely to our predetermined location.

Sometimes we have decided on a 90-day treatment program, which can sound like an eternity. When I know that may be objectionable, I prepare ahead of time. I might say something like, "We were thinking of this great 12- to 18-month treatment program, but now that I have met with you, I'm thinking that we can accomplish our goals in as little as 6 months or even 90 days." Now a 90-day program sounds like a preferred option and she feels as though she has had some part in the decision-making process. I might do the same with the location or length of aftercare, but I do not let her rule the conversation or terms. We have a plan. My job is to implement it and prepare the addicted loved one for it.

7. **Transportation**

Transportation is another important part of the process. Generally, I do not think it is wise for the family to transport the addicted loved one, because it is far too easy to be manipulated or get worn down. I can learn more about the addicted loved one during this time than any other. If a family member were present, that person might remain shut down, and that would interfere with our goals to communicate and develop a working relationship.

I always select driving rather than flying when possible. Airports and planes can be very stressful, not to mention that for some they provide the opportunity to act up at just the wrong moment and derail travel. Not only can they be detained at the airport by the authorities, but an expensive travel option can suddenly become much more expensive with new criminal charges or missed planes. I also think it is unwise to put someone on a plane unaccompanied. You have no real way of knowing he got on the plane, or if he changed his mind once at his destination airport. When air travel is unavoidable due to the distance of a particular treatment center, the tickets should be in first class. It means less congestion and fewer people to deal with in an already stressful situation. There are generally no children or infants in first class. It also provides convenient use of the bathroom if the client starts experiencing withdrawals. First class also means he will be the first one on and the first one off of the plane. There are typically only two seats on each side of the row, and the passenger receives much more attention from the flight attendant. This is much more expensive than coach, but it is safer for everyone involved. Driving is generally less stressful and less expensive. If time and distance permit, I prefer to drive.

8. Consequences

When the addicted loved one refuses help, you must stick to your guns and use the leverage you have. Your child may cry and beg you not to go through with it. Someone who loses everything and finds himself in a homeless shelter or jail, due to his own choices, may only need a very short time to come to his senses. Some may be stubborn and take much longer, but without any real consequences, there is little chance of change. We are trying to break his *addicted* spirit. He will almost always change his mind when he realizes that treatment can only help his case. Unwillingness to change and refusal of treatment plays out very poorly in court. I let him know that if the court decides he needs treatment, it will be court ordered and likely a program *within the prison system.* This can result in years of incarceration. In Texas, our prison treatment program, known as SAFP, is usually 6 to 9 months and frequently has a waiting list of 6 months to 1 year. This means he will wait in prison for a bed to open up, so there could be additional years added to the sentence. I always make sure he knows these facts to help leverage him into making better decisions. This makes me the guy who is helping him get out of jail and possibly avoid prison.

9. **Resolve**

You must have resolve, especially if the intervention does not go as planned. Your child may say horrible things to you, but you must know that it is the drugs or alcohol talking. They have taken your child hostage and you must win. I cannot emphasize this enough: *If you give in, the addiction wins and may take down your entire family.*

When I called my father for the second time

from jail he said, "I'm really sorry to hear that, son. Give us a call and let us know how everything worked out when you get out." Think about how difficult that was for him. I was young, stupid, and in the Dallas County Jail, which can be a very scary place.

The news never reports when people are treated well and are safe in jail; it only reports violence and corruption. Movies lead us to believe that all young men will be attacked and sexually assaulted. I'm not going to say that these things cannot happen, but remember that if we give into our fears, the behavior will continue and your child could end up in so much trouble that no amount of money or expert lawyers will keep her out of prison. Someone in prison for 20 years is much more likely to have problems with other inmates than someone who stays in a county jail for several months. This is all about changing the odds and increasing your child's chance of survival. I spent a lot of time in jail as a user and now I spend a lot of time in county jails to make contact with people I am working with. I have never heard about, seen, nor experienced a sexual assault in all those years.

10. Patience

Finally, you need patience. Even if the intervention lasts only minutes, and many of them do when well crafted, nothing changes overnight. Your child will not come home in 28 days completely fixed. Recovery is a long process and life is full of possible setbacks, including broken relationships, lost jobs, and wrecked cars.

You will need patience if your child is testing your resolve. This is heart-wrenching to say the least. Trust and rely on the professionals you have hired to do their job. If your child returns and continues the addictive behavior, reinstate your consequences and look for even more leverage. At this point, she knows how to get well and may only require detox and aftercare that includes PHP, IOP, and 12-step meetings. Sometimes patience and resolve are the only things you have, but they are indispensable.

COMMON PARTICIPANTS IN A SUCCESSFUL INTERVENTION

For an intervention to be successful, a variety of people must come together and work toward a common goal. The following section describes the people who are most likely to participate in a successful intervention.

1. **Family**

    This goes without saying. Without the support of the family, there is no intervention. No matter how bad your child's life may look like from the outside, he is getting his needs met somehow. His life, although admittedly not great, is working for him on some level or he would have asked for help. As stated earlier, sometimes we need to leave an individual family member out of the intervention because she will not stop enabling and may be in need of help herself.

2. Friends

Sometimes having friends involved is very powerful. The addict already trusts and confides in his friends, so if we can get them to help with the process we want them on our side. Even if we do not like or agree with the friends' lifestyle, if they are willing to help we want them as a part of the support system. For the purpose of the intervention, the support system is defined as a group of people who are willing to guide and hold someone accountable to achieve his goal of recovery. If they are not willing to help, leave them out of the intervention.

3. Employer

Chances are the employer is well aware of the situation and more than willing to make treatment and sobriety a condition of further employment. Some employers will even help provide treatment, but this is usually when someone has a professional career. If the employer is not willing to make further employment a condition of treatment and continued sobriety, we do not include him.

4. Spouse or Significant Other

Yes, one of my favorites. If we can get the spouse or love interest to agree to help (even if she is addicted too), we want to let her. Maybe she can be a part of our leverage. In your efforts to identify and understand the addict's possible objections, a love interest is at the top of the list. Sometimes there is fear that the love interest will not be there at the end of treatment. He does not want to leave her and often sees things as "us against the world," *especially if they're using together.* Sometimes, in an ideal outcome, we get both of them into some form of treatment. There are too many variations as to how this can play out to list, but again, this is where you follow the instincts of your interventionist.

You may hate the crazy addicted spouse or significant other, but I am going to ask you to put all of that aside for the benefit of your loved one. It may be difficult, and other family members may object; this is another one of those hard conversations you will want to have before the actual intervention. Remind your family that this is for the benefit of the entire family, whether they like it or not. I know what I am asking of you is not easy, but what has been easy so far? I have asked so much of you, and the fact that you are still here reading tells me that you can overcome this obstacle just as you have overcome everything else up to this point.

5. Attorney

If there is an attorney involved, you will want to include this person in your plans. He can often get your child to see certain things the family cannot. The lawyer speaks with authority, conviction, and objectivity. He has been down this road with clients many times and can shed light on what life will look like without change. I find attorneys to be excellent allies.

6. **Law Enforcement**

If there are warrants or a bail bond involved, I try to have the police close by. In my city, I have made it a point to develop a relationship with our police department, starting at the top and extending all the way down the chain of command to the patrol officers. I can usually call one of my friends and let him know what I am up to, so he can be available if needed. If I am in a city where I have no such relationships, I may or may not contact the police department ahead of time, depending on the circumstances. No matter where I am, they are just a call away and almost always willing to be helpful since they see more destruction from addiction than anyone else. At the end of the day, any police officer will take someone with warrants into custody.

7. **Court Representative**

This could be the judge, the prosecutor, the bailiff, the court administrator, or the defense counsel. Although these people can all play a part, it is the judge who can release someone for treatment and/or set the terms of the bond. Knowing all of this helps us develop the best possible plan of action. The court representative will not be at the intervention, but her role and input are crucial. Without the court, we may not be able to have bond set for releasing your child to treatment. We may also have the court make treatment a condition of his release, so refusing or leaving treatment results in an immediate return to jail.

EXAMPLES OF ACTUAL INTERVENTIONS

The following section describes real-life interventions in which I have been involved. I offer these as examples of the most common issues associated with interventions.

Example 1: Jailhouse Intervention
I start with this one as it is quick and simple. A friend of mine asked me to visit with someone in our county jail. He told me that his friends, the parents, wanted their son to go to treatment. As a favor, I stopped in and told the young man that he needed to go to treatment. I told him that I could get his parents to post bond but only if he was willing to go to treatment. Within five minutes he agreed, and I called my friend who arranged bail and transport with the parents. Although this was not contracted or paid, it was an intervention just the same. Jailhouse interventions are relatively easy because the choice is either to stay in jail or go to treatment. In this case, my friend was helping the family and already had a plan of action. All I did was drive a few miles to the county jail and talk for five minutes as a favor. I have done dozens of these informal interventions.

Example 2: Angry Mom
A woman called me for help with her daughter, who had already been to treatment numerous times but continued to use drugs. During our phone consultation, I quickly learned that the parents were incapable of saying no to their daughter. She explained that she had found used needles again and just didn't know what to do. She kept saying that I had to come get her daughter out of her house. She could not see that her own actions contributed to the lifestyle of her now 43-year-old daughter, so I asked her a simple question: "So, your

daughter is allowed to shoot heroin in your house?"

I will not repeat what came out of her mouth, but she was really mad at me and I thought she was going to hang up.

Me: Hang on. What did you find yesterday?
Mom: Used heroin needles.
Me: And was this the first time you ever found used heroin needles in your home?
Mom: God, no. I have been finding these damn things for years.
Me: And where is your daughter now?
Mom: She's upstairs . . . asleep.
Me: So you don't like it, but your daughter is allowed to shoot heroin in your house because otherwise she would be in jail or the homeless shelter.

The woman was not thrilled with me, but she did have to admit that she would not throw out her daughter or call the police. Whenever the daughter started working on her mom and dad, they would cave in and let her stay in the house. She now was using her own young son as leverage in the conflict, but this cycle had been going on for nearly three decades.

In short, I sent someone to check on the situation and then later spoke to the daughter on the phone. I let her know who I was and what I was going to do, and I asked her to pack her bag. I got her to agree to go with me early in the morning. When I arrived in the morning, she barely remembered our conversation, but I let her know that I wasn't leaving without her. About 30 minutes later, we were on our way to the detox hospital.

I present this example for two reasons:

1. The family was done spending money and could not afford expensive treatment. I informed the mother that the daughter had a number of dangerous drugs in her system and needed a medical detox at a cost between $5,000 and $7,000. If she wanted my help, this was a non-negotiable piece of the plan; it was not up for debate. From there, she was placed in our residential recovery program, which is a non-clinical, 12-step–based recovery program, where each individual goes to work and pays her own way. Although the family still had to pay for detox, first month's rent, and deposit, it was a plan they could afford. I had also mentioned a shelter in Dallas that would provide free detox and treatment services, but the mother would not hear of it and provided the necessary resources.

   The recovery program we provided, with a focus on independence, life skills, and accountability, was exactly what she needed. After talking with the woman, she agreed to follow our directions despite her many times in treatment and her arrogant attitude toward the subject.

2. Since the woman had been to treatment in excess of 20 times, she knew about treatment and what she had to do to stay sober. The problem was that without change in the home, there was no change. This woman had returned home and started using time after time. She had overdosed on more than one occasion, and so far had beaten the odds. I don't know how or why she was still alive, but she was. Now, many years after taking her to detox, she works for me, performing many

of our interventions. Because of her experiences, she has some of the greatest instincts I have come across.

Example 3: Interfering Family Member
At the initial family consultation/meeting, I discovered that the family was divided. They all wanted to help, but they mostly bickered and fought among themselves. It seemed as though the sister was trying to get everyone to call off the intervention because she didn't like the idea. She also told me, in an attempt to derail the intervention, that he was going to jail anyway so it did not matter what we did. She implied that she was trying to save her dad money, but she just didn't want a coordinated effort to get her little brother into treatment. Perhaps she was afraid of him getting well, or maybe she just wanted to be his friend and protector. The fact was that the father was holding all of the cards and didn't know it. He alone held the bond and was willing to revoke it at my request, despite what his daughter and ex-wife said.

After catching the sister in a number of lies, we confronted her and she apologized, but she continued to lie to us. She had contacted him through Facebook to warn him after telling us there was no way to reach him. After a short discussion, she gave me and my team her brother's cell phone number. How did we catch this? Drug addicts are not very smart while in their addiction; the young man made comments about his sister's warning on his Facebook timeline. My team immediately became aware of this, as Facebook provides an effective way to find out what someone is up to.

We realized that the father also paid for the son's phone, so we had it pinged to find his location. As it turned out, the sister knew where he was all along and seemed upset that we obtained his location. Without delay, we showed up to the motel in the next town and started texting.

"I'm here to take you to treatment."

No reply

"I'm here to take you to treatment, otherwise I am going to have to revoke your bond and have you arrested this morning."

His response: "I don't know where you think I am, but I'm not going anywhere."

"I'm right here at the motel, standing outside of your room."

A minute passed and then the shades pulled back and he looked out to see if we were really outside. Just as he looked out, a police car drove through the parking lot. This was a pretty seedy motel, and I waved at the officer and he waved back. Even though I have friends in this city's police department, I had not yet made a call. His appearance was purely a coincidence.

"It's time to come out and go with us or go with the police. You have five minutes or the deal is off and you go to jail where you will await trial for the next eight months. You can either get in our car or the squad car."

A few minutes later, he emerged from the room and was on his way to treatment. There were many reasons he might object to going with us, including a girlfriend and other friends, but we did not negotiate. He said that he called his sister and she would take him to treatment, but the terms were right now or jail; the sister was no longer part of the equation.

One of my team members escorted him. He was mad for the first two hours, but eventually he began to talk, and he actually thanked my team member when it was all said and done.

Example 4: Rich But Reluctant Son
A family contacted us about their adult son who had nearly unlimited funds available to him. Leverage seemed unlikely, so we had to appeal to his sense of family and his position in the family company. Because he was a partial owner, they could not take away his resources, but, following our direction, they did suspend him and told him he was temporarily barred from the company property.

My team member, who took the lead on this intervention, started texting him to no avail. We explained to the family our lack of leverage and asked for patience. Since the family followed our direction and refused to talk with their son—only responding with directions to contact my team member—he eventually texted back. The messages were vile, but it was communication nonetheless. My team member texted back and forth with him for more than three weeks. He blamed us for his life and for his family deserting him. She stayed on point and said that nothing about his situation would change until he was ready to go. She shared with him that I had done an intervention on her years earlier and knew exactly what he was going through. She said she hated me while it was happening, but now had a great life and she even worked for me. Eventually, he texted her and said that he was done and just wanted it to be over and go to treatment.

Having never met or even spoken on the phone, they set a time for her to pick him up. From there, they headed to the airport and then to treatment where he stayed for 90 days. He then attended a step-down program with the same treatment center for another 60 days. He only agreed to 28 days in the beginning, but he started to get well and wanted to stay. He and my team member are in touch to this day, and when he was struggling, he reached out to her. That's what rapport and credibility can do.

I chose these examples to demonstrate how each intervention can be different and how each situation calls for an individual plan. There are affordable treatment options and alternatives to fit any budget. If you are willing to jump through a few hoops or go to the Salvation Army, there are free options that are quite effective. Your child may not be on the beach or have any privacy, but she can receive lifesaving treatment.

Remember that an intervention involves leveraging someone to make a better decision. Once she agrees to go and makes it to her destination, the immediate intervention is 100% successful, but it is just a start. Ahead lie many decisions and actions, which we will look at in the next few chapters. An effective, solid intervention plan will include guidance and support during those crucial first months as well.

CHAPTER SIX

TREATING THE ADDICTION

In this chapter, I break down what treating addiction and the associated costs *really* look like. I explain how to successfully navigate your way in the industry and determine what the right moves are. Before you can make an educated decision, you must understand everything from level of care, co-occurring disorders, specialties, models, insurance, and aftercare. Without this knowledge, it is difficult and confusing to move ahead—another reason why a professional interventionist is a wise choice.

I love my industry. I love my organization. There are many people who are alive today because they came into contact with me or someone like me. My team and I spend much of our time educating families who have called us for help. Sometimes they are a fit and come directly into one of our programs, and other times their specific needs or situation are not appropriate for our facility. In these cases, we refer the family to a provider that fits their needs whom we know and trust. Like many in our industry, we just want to be helpful, even when it means we are not the right fit. For this reason, we have developed our own database of treatment providers who align with our ideology and culture.

You could say that as treatment providers we are all competitors, but a better description is that we are like a large family. We seek out relationships with providers across the country and catalog their specialties, pricing structures, accepted insurance policies, length of program, and treatment model. We see each other at conferences and trainings and tour each other's facilities. I am in Texas, but if a family calls and tells me their son must stay in another state, I can help.

As I write portions of this chapter, I am attending a conference to further my relationships within the treatment industry and keep everyone informed about our program. In other words, I am marketing my program while learning about other programs. These conferences also provide workshops that keep us up-to-date with the latest trainings and best practice theories. I say theories because the treatment industry is always evolving.

This can be confusing to a family that is suddenly faced with the fact that a child is in trouble and needs help. Sometimes the family's first instinct is to spare no expense, but spending more money does not always mean you are getting a better product.

WHAT ARE THE FACTS AND HOW MUCH IS THIS GOING TO COST?

I covered a lot of information about insurance in Chapter Three. I know most families have limited resources for treatment, especially if they have been down this road more than once. We just don't think about setting up a treatment fund for our children, as we would for an education, a car, or a wedding. As hard as this sounds, I am going to ask you to look at a couple of options to free up some resources.

Let's start by looking at the education fund. If you have set up an account for this, you may need to use the funds for treatment. If your child is using, attending college is no longer a given. Utilizing those funds to help him recover might make it possible that one day your child will be able to attend college. There are other ways to pay for school. If he continues to get high, college may be out of the picture anyway.

If there is no education fund available, maybe there is a car that could be sold to cover the costs. Obviously not your car or the family car, but if you have purchased a car for your child, selling it may help cover the costs. If you have set aside money in hopes of giving your child a fancy wedding, it may be time to reconsider that purpose. We want to keep your child alive long enough to have that dream come true someday.

There are associated costs involved with treatment. The following is a list of all available services to give you a complete picture. I have averaged the prices based on the industry. Once we look at all of the costs, we can look for ways to craft a treatment plan that fits your available resources. Keep in mind that your child may not need every one of the services I have listed.

Assessment with Drug/Alcohol Counselor	$150
Assessment with Psychiatrist	$300
Intervention	$5,000
Supervised Transport	$2,000
28-Day RTC or 90-Day RRC*	$30,000
Aftercare – PHP and IOP	$20,000
Counseling – 10 Sessions	$1,000
Structured Sober Living (3 months)	$3,000

* Residential treatment center or residential recovery center as described in Chapter Three

Wow! The total cost is just over $60,000!

Remember that if you have insurance you can cut the cost by $40,000 or more. If your child is willing to go to treatment when first confronted and you do not need a private assessment, intervention, or supervised transport, you can cut out another $7,300.

If the numbers are still too big and you have no insurance, you may look into state-funded treatment centers, religious programs, residential recovery programs, or payment plans for treatment. There are loans available specifically for this type of financial need.

The main idea is that we put together a plan you can afford without leaving out important components like aftercare and sober living. Perhaps residential treatment is not necessary or your child does not meet eligibility criteria. In this case, we would go straight to aftercare and a structured sober living program. There are still a number of costs associated with this plan; however, it is much more affordable.

Since residential treatment is by far the most expensive item on the list, let me break it down just a little further. We basically have four categories, which I will call luxury private pay, insurance dependent, state funded, and unlicensed recovery centers.

1. **Luxury Private Pay** – These are the high-end centers located in scenic areas with plush grounds and spa-like personal services. They may require a commitment of 30 to 90 days to complete their treatment model. Since they only accept cash payments, they do not have to answer to insurance companies or deal with coverage shortfalls. This ensures there will be no interruption of services or having a stay cut short.

   The costs associated with one of these luxury centers will range from $50,000 to $100,000 per month. Much like an exclusive country club, the price alone will ensure that a celebrity or sports figure will never be in treatment with someone from the working class. This treatment is designed for the rich and famous.

   Although these luxurious centers often have a great lineup of clinicians, it does not mean that clients are receiving better treatment or have increased odds of staying sober beyond treatment. The biggest difference is location and amenities. They are fabulous.

2. **Insurance Dependent** – The majority of treatment centers operate within this category. If you were to solely private pay, the costs would range from $15,000 to $40,000. The good news is that they accept insurance. Remember to contact your insurance company to find out exactly what benefits you have and how much they will cover. Even choosing an in-network facility can result in significant expenses depending on your deductible, coverage percentage, and out-of-pocket maximum. Since the insurance company will sometimes cut someone's benefits short, you need to know what the center will do in that case. Although your insurance company approves a program, it will not guarantee the length of stay. So even if it's a 28-day program, which is fairly standard, they may only approve 14 days of inpatient care. This is where "medical necessity" comes up again. There will be a review, usually weekly, to determine if insurance will continue to pay. Often insurance will not continue to cover at the inpatient rate and will only provide outpatient or partial hospitalization coverage. This leaves a substantial gap for the facility. *Make sure they do not use your aftercare benefits to extend or cover your child's stay unless you are prepared to pay for aftercare completely out-of-pocket.*

3. **State-Funded Centers** – These programs are always in great demand and often have a waiting list to get in. They can also be very difficult to qualify for. (This underscores why an interventionist with industry contacts can be extremely helpful.) These facilities are usually crowded and are often located in less desirable

areas. However, they very often provide solid treatment services by counselors and staff who are passionate about helping people. The main drawback with a state-funded program is the lack of education regarding spiritual development and growth, which I believe is far too important to leave out. If you don't have insurance or you cannot afford another treatment center, know that this is a very viable alternative. The whole idea of treatment is to separate someone from his surroundings and provide a very structured environment while treating whatever disorder is present. Once your child has completed treatment, you will want to be sure that a strong, 12-step–based aftercare program and structured sober living facility are a part of the plan.

4. **Unlicensed Recovery Centers** – In many cases, although unlicensed, these centers can be great alternatives for treatment as they are usually less expensive. Since there is no license or need to satisfy insurance companies, the center and staff are free to spend their efforts on their program. There are no credential requirements for staff, which makes operating expenses far less than that of a licensed treatment center. The staff is usually comprised of recovered alcoholics and addicts who are passionate about helping others.

    Unlicensed is not always a good thing and you don't want to start down this path with your eyes closed. Someone can typically stay in one of these centers for 90 days at around the same price as 30 days in a licensed residential treatment center. Before your child enters any unlicensed program, *you need to do your homework so you*

know what you are paying for. Call to ask about
the program and look for any print or online
reviews or references.

HOW DO WE KNOW WHERE TO GO?

Remember when we talked about who to call first?
Whether we called a hotline, a lawyer, or a clinician, or
met with an interventionist in person, we started the
selection process. If we had a private assessment
performed, we received a professional diagnosis to
consider. We should have received a few referral options
at the completion of the assessment. We have also
learned what level of care is appropriate.

Once you have a proper assessment, you can finalize the
process and select the facility that specializes in your
child's specific needs. For example, the trauma
experienced in a car accident and the trauma one might
experience in heavy combat are very different. Although
both individuals have experienced significant trauma, the
accident victim may not require the same level of care
that a wounded soldier requires; the treatment approach
will vary as well. When selecting an appropriate facility,
it is likely that the soldier will require a level of care that
can only be found in facilities that specialize in severe
trauma.

Many treatment centers will have a trauma program for
someone who requires a lower level of care. Since some
level of trauma is present in so many people with an
addiction, there are many well-qualified centers. But in
my opinion, there are only a handful of places that really
specialize in cases that involve the level of trauma one
would experience in combat or other extremely violent
events.

This same rule applies to eating disorders, personality disorders, self-harm, etc. There are wonderful facilities that specialize in each area.

There is no "one size fits all" when it comes to treatment. When you look at a 16-year-old male you can find a world of differences. Here are just a few things to consider:

- He may just be experimenting and was caught with a joint at school or alcohol at the lake. There is no full-blown addiction, but his problems must be addressed before they become bad habits.
- He may have started smoking pot at the age of 12 or younger and graduated to using heroin at 14. He is heavily addicted and in real trouble and at risk of a lethal overdose. The family may be unaware and cannot believe that their child is using a drug like heroin. This is currently the drug of choice of the upper middle class; you know, the right family in the right neighborhood, driving the right cars with expectations of their child attending the right university.
- He was put on ADD medications, which are amphetamines (speed) in most cases. He has started trading and selling various medications. The medications he has are legally prescribed, but he has been abusing them or selling them for something else. He too may be in grave danger.
- He attended a party, smoked pot, drank alcohol, and wrecked his car, which landed him in jail. This could be the first and only time he displays this type of behavior or it may just be the beginning. This is why you do not want to ignore the behavior or shield him from all consequences.

Remember that the legal drinking age is 21. This means drugs are often much easier to obtain than alcohol.

- He may have started using designer drugs, such as K2, Spice, or bath salts, to name just a few.

Something else you may wish to consider is distance. How far away from home is safe? What is too far away and what is too close? Consider this example from my own professional experience.

I was once told that two days after a man took his daughter to treatment she showed up at home. He was angry about the money he spent just for her to show up at home. When I asked how far away they lived from the treatment center, he told me they lived less than two miles from the center and she walked home.

I suggested he try a center much farther away from home to remove that option. He then told me that her friends would drive to Austin, Texas, to get her. So I asked about Lubbock, a city located in the Texas Panhandle.
There is a treatment center there that fit every need. It didn't need to be all the way across the country, but it did need to be far enough away that her friends wouldn't come and pick her up. No one wants to drive six hours from Dallas to Lubbock, especially the friends of a teenage girl. Her friends may be willing to drive to Austin because it's closer and is a city known for music and a good time.

WHAT ABOUT SPECIALTIES OR CO-OCCURRING DISORDERS?

"Co-occurring disorder" is a term that is used when there

is more than one diagnosis or issue. Sometimes we have a substance abuse issue combined with a mental health issue such as depression, bipolar disorder, or anxiety. Sometimes it's "process" addictions, such as sex, eating disorders, or gambling.

What I want you to understand is this: All of these disorders feed off of each other. We often spend too much time attempting to decipher which came first or which caused the other. Possibly the mental health issue is feeding the addiction, and possibly the addiction is feeding the mental health issue. To keep this simple, let's just agree that for the purpose of this discussion, it does not really matter.

The fact is that they simultaneously exist and must both be treated. If we treat just the mental health issue and not the addiction, the likely result will be that the untreated addiction will run its course of problems and consequences, leading the individual right back into crisis and exacerbating the mental health issue. Using this same logic, if we treat the addiction and not the mental health issue, it will again rear its ugly head. Whether depression, bipolar, or personality disorder, it will lead the individual back to self-medicating. This is how he has learned to cope, which reactivates the addiction.

It's a vicious cycle that must be addressed. Not everyone with a mental health issue has a substance abuse issue and not every addiction comes with a mental health disorder, but the numbers are pretty clear on this.

Let me paint this in a different light and look at this as one big, all-inclusive disorder that must be treated. Let's just say the addicted loved one is sick.

If you were injured in a car crash, you wouldn't see a different doctor or visit a different hospital for each broken bone. It may require a number of procedures over time with different specialists, but you would treat the whole body right from the start. It may be that some of your injuries are more significant or complicated than others and require more attention with follow-up appointments or additional procedures.

Co-occurring disorders are no different. You cannot ignore one issue and expect a positive outcome any more than you can ignore a broken leg because it wasn't life-threatening at the moment.

To provide further insight into and understanding of the issues related to co-occurring disorders, I offer the following example of a family I worked with.

A man brought his daughter to us one day hoping she would meet the criteria for our residential program. When they arrived, some of my team took the young woman into an interview room. Here was a 20-year-old woman who was covered in scratches and various bruises. I noticed that the white of one eye was completely red from a recent eye injury. A few minutes later, I walked into the room and the woman started trembling and looked straight at the ground. Something about my presence, as the only male in the room, was causing her distress. I backed out of the room without saying a word.

She looked much like Ashley Judd after her character escapes from her captor in the movie *Kiss the Girls*. And much like the character portrayed in that movie, the young woman in my office sustained her injuries running through the woods as she escaped her captors. She had been missing for two weeks, during which time she was held captive and sexually assaulted by multiple assailants. She had returned home just a day earlier, and now here she was sitting in my office.

Most members of my team have personally experienced many traumatic experiences; however, when they reported to me what the young woman said, they were genuinely shaken up. Upon hearing the traumatic details of what had taken place, I pulled the father to the side to explain the need for intensive treatment that specialized in this type and level of trauma.

His reply was shocking and infuriating, "What? Did she tell you about her story in the woods? I'm not sure if I believe all that or not."

Seeing red, I tried to remain as calm as possible, and I told this man the following: "Whether you believe her or not, your daughter has obviously been through some sort of traumatic experience. Someone has physically beaten your daughter from head to toe. She has obviously run through the woods and has experienced something violent and terrifying. Even if she is fuzzy on the details, she has suffered a significant trauma that needs to be addressed immediately. In my opinion, there are just a handful of centers in the country that are equipped for this level of trauma, and we are not able to admit her until this has been addressed."

He replied, "How much is all of this going to cost?"

Again, I tried to remain calm and explain to him that until this was addressed, all other forms of treatment were pointless; no respectable center would disagree or admit her without addressing the trauma. "This is going to be expensive, but if you ever want your daughter to get past this, you're going to have to open up your checkbook or take out a loan to address it."

Sometimes I am able to help people see the wisdom in following certain directions, and in this case I was able to help the father see that ignoring this would cost much more in the long run. Just a few hours later they were on a plane headed to a facility that was well equipped to help her heal.

Understanding treatment, and what approach is the right one, can be as simple as starting with a consultation. It can be very expensive, depending on one's needs, but there is something at greater risk than money.

Most reputable agencies or centers will do the right thing. For example, we referred the young woman to the appropriate center, which happened to be across the country. She did not return nor did we make any money from her family. She was beyond of our level of expertise and we made a call that was in her best interest. I know that there are people with bad intentions selling snake oil out there, but I believe that the majority of people in my profession are here to help.

IDEOLOGY AND MODELS OF TREATMENT

In this section, I discuss key terms and concepts related to the treatment process.

Ideology refers to the basic belief structure in which a substance abuse treatment or recovery organization operates. This sets the tone for how all activities are carried out and connect on some level.

I once visited a treatment center for a professionals' weekend where we were able to meet the staff, tour the properties, and take part in some of the activities offered to their clients. My favorite activity involved wearing a safety harness and then jumping from a dam while attempting to fully extend my arms and legs instead of holding onto the cables. This is a form of experiential therapy. The point of the exercise was a blind leap of faith, letting go of everything and jumping, feeling completely exposed.

This is where it ties in to their ideology. The Third Step of 12-step programs says that we made a decision to turn our will and our lives over to the care of God as we understood Him. This is a leap of faith. At this point we do not really understand God or how this is going to help us stop using. We do it because we have come to believe that there is a Power greater than ourselves that has helped others and just might be able to help us. It is the point where we jump off into the work and start taking action. Since this treatment center is based in the Twelve Steps, this ties every activity to one step or another. Jumping off of a dam was just a physical action of taking this leap of faith. A counselor sat with each of us to say the Third Step prayer before we jumped to make sure we made the connection.

Models refers to a specific approach used in treatment. There are numerous models, but for the purpose of this chapter I will explain the most common models in use. Note that *in my opinion,* treatment without a 12-step model is missing the most important aspect of recovery.

Harm Reduction is a set of practical strategies and ideas aimed at reducing negative consequences associated with drug use. Much of this involves the idea of meeting the addicts where they are. Programs include needle exchanges, education, counseling, and drug replacement therapies that include Suboxone and methadone.

This is a non-judgment approach where counselors may freely share their beliefs but are not allowed to make judgments for the client. There is a belief that some people will never achieve total abstinence, and, therefore, the goal is to help the client find a safer level of living. The idea behind drug replacement therapy is to deliver a cleaner drug to keep the addict from experiencing withdrawals and possibly help him be able to lead a more productive life, hence the name harm reduction. There are many men and women who are able to lead safer and more productive lives utilizing a harm reduction model; however, they are still dependent on drugs and the clinic that provides them. Withdrawal from these drugs is often more painful and dangerous than the withdrawal experienced from heroin.

I have mixed emotions about this as, *in my opinion,* this is just kicking the ball downfield. To be completely fair, here are two positive examples of harm reduction.

Example 1 – There is a man in South Chicago who runs a needle exchange program right out of his mobile clinic. He drives around the areas in South Chicago that aremost affected by heroin use, which are also areas with a high crime rate. While handing out clean needles, he provides education about cleaner living and how to keep down the transmission of diseases through intravenous drug use.

What I most appreciate about this man is he also carries

the lifesaving drug Naloxone (Narcan) in his truck, which, when administered in time, immediately reverses the effects of an opioid overdose. He makes sure everyone who participates in the needle exchange program has his cell number. I have no idea how many lives he has saved, but whenever someone asks for help, he is right there to get the addict into a treatment program. For this reason, he is a hero in the industry.

Example 2 – I have a friend in Texas who is part of the harm reduction model through his work at a methadone clinic. Although I do not see eye to eye with him about the drug, he is responsible for helping thousands of men and women. In order to participate at his clinic, the clients must receive counseling and education about addiction. When someone makes the decision to transition to complete abstinence, he is there to help and support them. For this reason, I have nothing but respect for my friend.

Cognitive Behavioral Therapy (CBT) is a short-term, goal-oriented, psychotherapy treatment that takes a hands-on, practical approach to problem-solving. Its goal is to change the patterns of thinking or behavior that are behind people's difficulties as a means to change the way they feel. The therapist and client work together as a team to identify and solve problems.

This model has many practical uses and is most often used to treat a variety of mental health disorders. It is based on the belief that thought distortions and maladaptive behaviors play a role in the development and maintenance of psychological disorders.

Many treatment centers offer CBT in conjunction with the 12-step model when treating co-occurring disorders.

In my opinion, CBT alone does not make for an effective drug and alcohol treatment model. I feel it is important to say that CBT can look very different, depending on the application.

Rational Recovery was developed by a licensed social worker in the 1980s who was battling his own addiction to alcohol. Unlike traditional 12-step models such as Alcoholics Anonymous, Rational Recovery does not have a spiritual component; it is based in self-reliance. The idea is that once you are able to manage the "Addicted Voice" within, there is no need for additional steps.

To be completely fair, and this is *my opinion*, this model may offer help to someone who has just dabbled with drugs and does *not* have an addiction. This completely contradicts the idea that we must treat the body, mind, and soul. I am aware of a certain adolescent program that utilizes this model, but I have never met anyone who beat their addiction using this program.

There are two other treatment models you should know about. There was a program that claimed to cure alcoholism in two weeks using a drug that made someone violently ill when combined with alcohol. The idea was to take the drug and drink alcohol for two weeks with the intended outcome that people would be so sick from alcohol they would never drink again. This approach echoes the idea that if you ever got really sick from a certain food you would never want to eat it again. The mere thought would induce a gagging reflex that would ensure that response. I will give them an "A" for effort because I love this kind of out-of-the-box thinking. The problem was that an alcoholic understood that once the drug was out of his system he could drink without getting sick. I do have a good friend in the treatment industry who went through this program in the 1980s. Since he completed the program, he has never been able to drink gin; however, this is when he started drinking bourbon.

There are presently one or more treatment centers that claim to be able to cure addiction. They pointedly advertise they are *not* a 12-step program. They claim that once you learn how to control the urge to use, you are cured. Some of these centers have effective marketing strategies, but participants pay a great deal of money to attend their luxurious facilities, where they receive services from masseuses, chefs, and mystics instead of formally trained counselors or medical staff.

Unlike the unlicensed residential recovery centers that offer 12-step immersion as a cost-effective alternative to residential treatment, *in my opinion,* this model preys upon wealthy families who desperately want to put the whole episode of addiction behind them in one shot. The promise of a cure is often contingent upon entering into a long-term contract with one of their counselors, at the cost of $60,000 per month after the initial cost of $85,000 per month to visit the center.

Before I discuss the 12-step model, I want to encourage you to question my findings and do your own research. If there was only one way people could get better, there would only be one treatment center, re-created all over the world. As a student of the 12-step program, I believe that however one attempts to recover, there MUST be treatment for body, mind, *and* spirit, as well as help for the entire family. Addiction is a systemic family disorder and MUST be treated as such.

THE 12-STEP MODEL

This approach is also known as the Disease Model, the Minnesota Model, the Abstinence Model, and the Blended Model. Although the 12-step and disease names are self-explanatory, Minnesota is where the model was first developed, and the term Blended refers to the blending of professionals and nonprofessionals who utilize clinical strategies with the 12-step program principles.

The model was created in a state mental hospital in the 1950s by two young men, one who was to become a psychologist, the other who was to become a psychiatrist. Neither of them had prior experience treating addicts or alcoholics. The model spread first to a small not-for-profit organization called the Hazelden Foundation and then throughout the country.

The key element of this novel approach to addiction treatment is the blending of professional and trained nonprofessional (recovering) staff around the principles of Alcoholics Anonymous (AA). This approach features an individualized treatment plan with active family involvement in a 28-day inpatient setting and participation in AA both during and after treatment. The education of patients and family about the disease of addiction makes this a busy program from morning to night, seven days a week.

This model is the basis for most residential treatment programs. It is a comprehensive, multidisciplinary approach to the treatment of addictions that is abstinence-based and grounded in the principles of Alcoholics Anonymous. It includes group therapy, lectures, counseling by clinicians and recovering persons, multidisciplinary staff, a therapeutic milieu, therapeutic work assignments, family counseling, the use of a 12-step program, daily reading (Twelve Step literature) groups, the presentation of a life history, attendance at 12-step meetings and the opportunity for recreation and physical activity. These elements are generally integrated into a structured daily routine. Local 12-Step groups provide the mainstay of the aftercare phase.

Let's break this down to provide an understanding of the twelve steps, spiritual principles, and some of the 12-step promises. My intentions here are to clear up any misunderstandings about the 12-step model.

The Twelve Steps: These come from AA, but sufferers using another drug or who have a process addiction can just substitute the appropriate term in place of alcohol (e.g., cocaine, heroin, gambling, sex).

1. **We admitted we were powerless over alcohol that our lives had become unmanageable.**
   This happens the moment we realize that we are in big trouble with our addiction and we need help. Since this is nothing more than an admission to self, there is no action to be taken. However, if one does not believe he is completely and hopelessly powerless over his addiction, little to no progress can be made. Typically, someone who does not believe he has a problem will not do the intense spiritual and emotional work to come. Sometimes we just need someone to help us to see how our present circumstances (e.g., jail sentence, trouble at work or school, trouble with relationships) are a direct result of using drugs or alcohol.

The litmus test is if, when you honestly want to, you find you cannot quit entirely or if when drinking you have little control over the amount you take, you are probably an alcoholic. (Basic Text, pg. 44)

2. **Came to believe that a Power greater than ourselves could restore us to sanity.**
This is another realization that happens when we come into contact with a recovered person who shares her past and how she got well. It is the hope that if this person could get well despite everything she did, maybe the person still suffering could do the same. Often this is her first encounter with someone who speaks her own language and truly understands what she is going through. Up to this point, she may have been told to "Just say NO" or been scolded about being better than the addiction. Preaching has never worked. Perhaps this will, since the person carrying the message of hope to her has no more power than she does—and yet something has absolutely transformed him, something that is obviously more powerful than either of them.

3. **Made a decision to turn our will and our lives over to the care of God *as we understood Him.***
This is a hugely misunderstood step. It is the leap of faith we have talked about. At this point, most of us have no real idea who God is, or we are closed off to the idea altogether. There is an entire chapter in the Basic Text devoted to this, titled "We Agnostics."

This is also the step that many of my religious

friends have a problem with, as they feel there is only one God and making a reference to anything else is unacceptable. I have heard statements like, "My problem with the whole thing is this Anything Goes, or Coke Machine God." I always explain that almost no one is sitting in church when he decides he needs to take care of his addiction. He is often living in hell on earth, and believes that if there is a God, He has forgotten or forsaken him. His addiction is the biggest and most powerful thing in his life and he simply does not have the capacity to understand anything else.

There is also the fact that the person asking for help may have not had a religious upbringing or know anything about God. Possibly he comes from another religion and is not willing to change his entire belief structure. Regardless of our religious beliefs, are we not charged with helping our neighbor? You know, "Love thy neighbor as thyself." It doesn't say help only those who agree with you. We are charged with helping anyone and everyone whom we are able.

Let's look at exactly what the Basic Text of A.A. says about this. We find that God does not make the terms too hard for those who seek Him. The realm of the Spirit is never forbidding to those who earnestly seek. It is open, we believe, to all men. (Basic Text, pg. 46) I personally know many men and women who were far from the church, but who have returned as a direct result of this program, including myself. Even if someone never enters any house of worship, we are still charged with helping him.

Here we take our first action, when ready, and recite the Third Step prayer with the person who is helping us, our sponsor. The following is the Third Step prayer: "God, I offer myself to You— to build with me and to do with me as You will. Relieve me of the bondage of self, that I may better do Your will. Take away my difficulties, that victory over them may bear witness to those I would help of Your Power, Your Love, and Your Way of life. May I do Your will always!"

4. Made a searching and fearless moral inventory of ourselves.

We are to complete three different lists to make up this fearless moral inventory. First, we list our resentments, why we have them, and what we believe they have affected. Second, we make another list of our fears, why we have them, and what we believe they have affected. At this time, we may not be able to see our fears, but that will be addressed in the next step. Third, we make a list of our sex conduct, explaining who we have hurt and what we did. If we are able see it, we also add what we believe that has affected.

This step should not take long, nor is it hard once you get started on it. The biggest challenge is that people are often unwilling to look at their own behaviors; sometimes they do not see how this has anything to do with their addictions. Here is the leap of faith. We do this because the person who has given us hope said that we MUST do this to get well. We are not to over-analyze the process. We simply make our inventory without having to understand why.

5. **Admitted to God, to ourselves, and to another human being the exact nature of our wrongs.**

   This is when we go over our lists with our sponsor, whose job is to help us see our truths. It is a fact-finding mission to discover why we get mad, why we use our sexuality to manipulate others, and why we have certain fears. As we complete our first list, we learn that most of our actions are driven by fear, especially when we are angry. Sometimes we have a hard time seeing this; men, especially, are wired to believe we are fearless, that anything less would be unmanly. The truth is that we act the way we do because we are afraid of many things: that we won't get our way, that others won't look at us as we want, that we will not get enough, and that we will not be treated as we feel we deserve. We MUST fully understand this concept before moving forward. Many of us, myself included, entered this step thinking we were going to assign blame to others and justify our actions, but we could not.

6. **Were entirely ready to have God remove all these defects of character.**

   Once we finish Step Five, we are supposed to return home and spend one hour alone considering our work so far. We ask ourselves if we have been as honest as we can and if we have done the work thus far to the best of our abilities. If we can answer these questions to our own satisfaction, we are ready to move on to Step Seven. If we feel we have missed something, we contact our sponsor immediately and go over what we have missed.

As we go through our lives, God will continually reveal more to us. Not to worry. There are steps further down the list considered our "maintenance steps," where we are able to deal with such revealed issues. We are human and therefore we will make future mistakes and wrong people again. These maintenance steps are designed to help us deal with our daily human condition.

7. Humbly asked Him to remove our shortcomings.
When ready, we recite the Seventh Step prayer. Many regard it as the second half of the Third Step prayer, as we are now more aware and have gained understanding of what we are praying for.

The following is the Seventh Step prayer: "My Creator, I am now willing that You should have all of me, good and bad. I pray that You now remove from me every single defect of character which stands in the way of my usefulness to You and my fellows. Grant me strength, as I go out from here, to do Your bidding. Amen." This completes Step Seven. (Basic Text, pg. 76)

8. Made a list of all persons we had harmed, and became willing to make amends to them all.
We actually have this list; we made it when we listed our resentments and sex conduct, although we may need to add additional names of people we wronged who do not fit in either of those categories. This step should take no more than an hour to complete.

Let me now address a common myth about the 12 steps. Many have been told that the steps take a minimum of a year to complete, but as you can see, the steps are nothing more than a series of exercises that are designed to be worked quickly. True happiness and the freedom we are promised come from working all 12 steps. Why would we ever want people to wait a year before they found relief from their addictions? This misunderstanding has even claimed the lives of some men and women. If you were so desperate that you considered taking your life just to end the pain and noise of life, would you be willing to wait a year to get any real relief?

9. **Made direct amends to such people wherever possible, except when to do so would injure them or others.**
   This we do under the care and guidance of our sponsor. Some of the people on our list will not be happy to see us, and an already ugly situation may get worse. If we have expectations about how others should treat us just because we are working a program, we are setting ourselves up for resentment. When we harbor resentments or continue to treat others poorly, we are in grave danger of relapse. We MUST enter this step with our eyes open and be willing to take whatever criticism others have to offer. These are our amends to make, not theirs. We simply go to each person on our list, explain that we have wronged them, and ask what we can do to right the wrong. We then close our mouths and listen. We do our very best to carry out whatever errand they have asked of us, unless it is unreasonable or might harm someone.

We will experience more spiritual growth as we carry out this step than any other time in our recovery and possibly our lives.

10. Continued to take personal inventory and when we were wrong promptly admitted it.

This is the first of our maintenance steps, we continue to work closely with our sponsor anytime we are angry or agitated, find ourselves becoming selfish, treat others poorly, or are confused about what to do next. I have been clean and sober from my addictions since 1995. To this day, whenever I am unsettled or considering a major change in my life, I contact my sponsor and run the facts by him. One of our AA promises is that we will intuitively know how to handle situations that used to baffle us, but it does not say we will never again be baffled. Although we grow in understanding and are less frequently baffled, we keep these relationships with our sponsors so that when we need direction, it is available.

11. Sought through prayer and meditation to improve our conscious contact with God *as we understood Him*, praying only for knowledge of His will for us and the power to carry that out.

This is pretty straightforward stuff, and there are hundreds of books written on the subject of prayer and meditation; however, I have never read anything as simple and powerful as the direction found in the Basic Text concerning this. I urge you to pick up a copy, or at least go online and read pages 87–89.

12. **Having had a spiritual awakening as the result of these steps, we tried to carry this message to alcoholics and to practice these principles in all our affairs.**

What a great challenge! Having had a spiritual awakening as a result of the work, we are now to go and help others, by being that person who brings hope and help to the suffering addict. If he accepts it, we become his sponsor and take him through the work. We make this a part of our lives; we stay spiritually fit by practicing our spiritual principles and making time to help others. Others will be drawn to us as someone with a real solution to the problems of life. This does not mean we will never again experience hardships; it means we will know how to deal with them so they will not become resentments.

What Are the Promises? The following are the promises we shall each receive as we complete the steps.

- We are going to know a new freedom and a new happiness.

- We will not regret the past nor wish to shut the door on it.

- We will comprehend the word serenity and we will know peace.

- No matter how far down the scale we have gone, we will see how our experience can benefit others.

- That feeling of uselessness and self-pity will

disappear.

- We will lose interest in selfish things and gain interest in our fellows.

- Self-seeking will slip away.

- Our whole attitude and outlook upon life will change.

- Fear of people and of economic insecurity will leave us.

- We will intuitively know how to handle situations which used to baffle us.

- We will suddenly realize that God is doing for us what we could not do for ourselves.

The following lists the **Spiritual Principles** we use to guide our lives.

- **HONESTY** – Fairness and straightforwardness of conduct; adherence to the facts.

- **HOPE** – To expect with desire; something on which hopes are centered.

- **FAITH** – Complete confidence; belief and trust.

- **COURAGE** – Firmness of mind and will in the face of extreme difficulty; mental or moral strength to withstand fear.

- **INTEGRITY** – The quality or state of being complete or undivided; soundness.

- **WILLINGNESS** – Prompt to act or respond; accepted and done of choice or without reluctance.

- **HUMILITY** – Not proud or haughty; not arrogant or assertive; a clear and concise understanding of what we are, followed by a sincere desire to become what we can be.

- **LOVE** – Unselfish concern that freely accepts another in loyalty and seeks his good to hold dear.

- **DISCIPLINE** – Training that corrects, molds, or perfects the mental faculties or moral character; to bring under control; to train or develop by instruction.

- **PATIENCE/PERSEVERANCE** – Steadfast despite opposition or adversity; able or willing to bear; to persist in an understanding in spite of counter influences.

- **AWARENESS** – Alive and alert; vigilance in observing.

- **SERVICE** – A helpful act; contribution to the welfare of others; useful labor that does not produce a tangible commodity.

We are not perfect, and so we keep these principles imperfectly. This is what we are striving for. It's actually quite simple: do the work, trust God, help others, and try to do the right thing.

At the end of this book I have included additional information from the Basic Text of Alcoholics Anonymous. See pages 226–230 of Appendix III.

THE ADMISSION PROCESS

Initial Call – If inpatient treatment is the appropriate level of care, and the appropriate treatment center has been selected, an assessment will be performed by the treatment center during the initial call.

There are two parts to the initial call:

1. Before the treatment center does an assessment with the addicted loved one over the phone, you need to address and secure funding. The treatment center will want to speak to the person who is going to pay for treatment or the person who is the insurance policyholder and is responsible for out-of-pocket expenses. At the time of your family crisis, this portion of the call may feel cold and institutional; however, treatment is expensive and they first need to determine eligibility. I don't think there is an easy way to do this, but there are some people who are gifted in this area and others who make the process feel unpleasant. If you are utilizing insurance, you will need to provide the policy number and the group number, as well as the policyholder's name, birthdate, and social security number.

   This part of the process can be frustrating as you wait to hear back from the insurance company. The treatment center will conduct a verification of benefits with the insurance company after they have collected all of the necessary information. There is no rhyme or reason why sometimes this process is quick and other times it takes far too long. It can feel like buying a car over the phone.

If there are any out-of-pocket expenses, they will let you know the amount and make arrangements to collect payment for them. Remember to ask what will happen if the insurance company only approves a portion of treatment and declines the rest. Remember that inpatient treatment is just the beginning of the journey. If you are using insurance, you will need your aftercare benefits for that vital phase of treatment.

Note that when an intervention is performed, this portion of the initial call has already taken place.

2. The second portion of the initial call is the assessment to make sure the addicted loved one has met criteria and treatment is a medical necessity. Depending on how coherent and forthcoming the addicted loved one is, this could take anywhere from 30 minutes to an hour or more. The treatment center will ask what drugs he is currently using, how much he is using, how long it has been since his last use, and if he is experiencing withdrawal or other side effects. They will also ask many questions about his drug and alcohol use history, and if he has ever received treatment, a diagnosis, or services for any mental health disorders. After these criteria are met, he is approved for admission. Once he arrives, they will check vitals and continue with the assessment for any missing information.

After Admission – Once admitted, the addicted loved one will enter the detox phase of treatment, if necessary, which will last anywhere from three to seven days. As soon as he is able to start attending group therapy, he is usually encouraged to do so, even though he may not yet be completely detoxed.

Once he is part of the general population, he will start the structured activities, begin individual and group counseling, and take part in a number of experiential therapy activities. There is also a physical fitness component. During residential treatment, every hour of every day is structured to include activities and clinical processes that all tie into the treatment center's ideology, methodology, and treatment model.

Since each treatment center has its own personality and area of expertise, I have remained vague about specific activities. Some centers utilize activities such as rope courses, zip lines, leap of faith jumps, work with animals, sweat lodges, storytelling, expressive art therapy, expressive music therapy, letter writing to the addiction, or inner child workshops. The list can be much longer and is only limited by the imagination of the treatment center staff.

Treatment centers may specialize in trauma, eating disorders, gambling, sex addiction, anxiety, depression, bi-polar disorder, codependency, personality disorders, and other compulsive behavior disorders. There are some centers that have a complete medical department to be able to provide treatment for life-threatening injuries or diseases. For example, if someone is treated for an eating disorder and needs a feeding tube, she requires a center that looks more like a hospital. The same is true for someone with cirrhosis of the liver, failing kidneys, etc.

AFTERCARE

This stage of recovery may look like PHP (Partial Hospitalization Programs), IOP (Intensive Outpatient Treatment Programs), continued counseling, or a structured sober living or transitional program. This is where those who have been in treatment will learn the basic life skills necessary for a life of abstinence. Remember that drugs and alcohol have become their coping mechanism and they must learn how to stand on their own two feet.

No matter which programs are involved, I cannot emphasize this enough: Aftercare is just as important as inpatient treatment.

Like any other disease, recovery from an addiction requires a complete change in one's lifestyle. After a heart attack, you don't want to return to the old behaviors that caused the issue, so why would you let your child return to the same environment or activities that led to her issue? Sometimes we are part of that problem and must make changes in our own behavior. The need for change within the family is one of the most difficult aspects of recovery, but it is also one of the most important. The next chapter in this book is intended to address this part of the process.

I have received several calls from upset parents who claimed that their children received bad or ineffective treatment. As I spoke to each of these parents, I learned that they all had one thing in common: their children never completed or submitted to aftercare. Usually these children were allowed back into the family home where, not surprisingly, they returned to the same activities that led to their troubles in the first place.

We would walk through each complaint about the various centers, and I would explain that I knew the center and was sure that their child had not received bad treatment. The real problem was that they did not follow directions. Sometimes the family drove back to the center to remove their child, against medical advice, because their child called and said that she did not want to stay. In every case, the treatment center insisted on aftercare, and the family ignored the wise counsel they received. Usually they claimed the center was just trying to get them to spend more money. This is untrue. Treatment that does not include a comprehensive aftercare plan is destined to fail.

I may sound like a broken record, but I am going to tell you this again: We know that the longer one is in a structured environment the better her chances are.

CHAPTER SEVEN

GETTING OUT OF THE WAY: THE MOST DANGEROUS TIME

I cannot say that one chapter is more important than the next; they are all important and I have presented them in a specific order, each chapter building on the next. There are certain ideas that you will come to after learning what the prior chapters have taught you. You cannot skip one chapter and expect to have the desired outcome. This chapter is *crucial*, provided you have studied each chapter leading up to this point.

The most dangerous time for everyone suffering from an addiction is right after a high level of accountability is removed. For some, it is the moment they walk out of jail, and for others it is the moment they walk out of treatment. Although the accommodations are quite different, it's the same thing. Doors that were locked are now open, and they head out into the world, *ready or not*.

You want to believe that your child is well, or has learned a valuable lesson that will keep her from temptation. You desperately want to put this episode behind you, forget about it, and move on as a family.

When we walk back into the world, we may have the best of intentions, but we're very susceptible to falling into old habits. The change can be so subtle that we don't even see it happening. Before we know it, we have placed ourselves in a compromising situation that pulls us back into a world of pain and consequences. One moment we are having dinner with Mom and the next we are fighting for life in another ambulance or headed to jail. How quickly and far we can fall with just one misstep.

So many times I sat in the Dallas County Jail awaiting release, and I always resolved that I would never return. Left to my own devices, I had four to six months before everything would fall apart and I would find myself back in jail again. I couldn't tell you why or what would happen leading up to the arrest; I just knew that somehow I would shoot myself in the foot. Now when I visit jails I am told the very same thing by so many. When I have the opportunity, I share how I always found more trouble after having those same thoughts. I explain how one thing always led to another, and before I knew it everything would be bad again. At this point, the majority of them come clean and admit that they always do the same thing.

They were not lying about their desire to never return to that life; they meant every word and believed it with every fiber of their being. They were just unprepared for the *reality of the free world*.

I always ask the same three questions:
1. Do you know where you are going to live?
2. Do you know where you are going to eat?
3. Do you know where you are going to work?

These questions seem simple enough and we just assume that these things will fall into place. Often we have forgotten the details surrounding our past behaviors, and we can't imagine that our friends and family might not want us in their homes, or that we aren't welcome to return to our place of employment.

Even when I'm able to land on my feet, there are pressures. Just to legally drive a car, I must take care of automotive insurance, inspection stickers, a valid license, and valid registration tags. I know that everyone has to deal with this, but while in treatment or jail, we did not. We were fed, clothed, housed, and cared for; we had no responsibilities or bills. Often, prior to getting sober, we hadn't taken care of the necessities of life for ourselves, and we didn't care if our insurance was current or our license was valid. Now it's a whole new game, and suddenly the weight of the world is on our shoulders as we walk out into a situation for which we are unprepared. In our program, we often see 40-year-olds who have never done a load of laundry, refilled a prescription, or written a check that didn't bounce.

There are those who are so afraid to leave the safety of treatment or jail that they act out in hopes of staying longer. They would *never* admit that, but it's true. That fear can be overwhelming. Intentional or not, consciously or unconsciously, they sabotage themselves, derailing their own progress and starting the cycle all over again. Until they have learned how to live and develop new coping mechanisms, they will always be at risk.

WHAT AFTERCARE LOOKS LIKE

There are many different options for aftercare. Ultimately, your choice will depend on the specific needs of your child. Here is an overview of the most common types of treatment centers.

PHP – A Partial Hospitalization Program is the level of care just below inpatient treatment. The patient remains in treatment for five to eight hours a day, five days a week, usually while residing in a controlled environment, such as a structured residential recovery program or structured sober living. In some instances, he may live at home during this process. It can be the first phase of moving from inpatient treatment back into the community. Contact with friends and family may be limited as his attention is focused on the reintegration process.

IOP – Typically, this outpatient treatment program runs three hours a night, three or four nights a week. The patient returns to work and has full contact with friends and family. I believe it is best that during this process she remains in a residential recovery program, such as sober living, although it is not mandated. A patient in IOP may return home, but I don't recommend it.

Individual Counseling – During inpatient treatment, PHP, and IOP, the client receives a number of individual counseling sessions. Often this continues for a period of time beyond IOP.

Each client and each situation will be different. I recommend that if your child is making good progress with his counselor, let the sessions continue for as long as necessary. The more support and accountability, the better. Follow the clinician's recommendations regarding length of treatment.

Structured Sober Living – Just as it sounds, this is a residential recovery program for people in early sobriety. In a strong, well-structured sober housing organization, there are expectations to comply with rules, move through a level system that tracks one's progress, return to the workforce, and take part in many educational opportunities. No two programs look alike, but what you are looking for is a strong 12-step component, structure, and accountability. These programs are designed to have someone walk side by side with a recovering addict while he learns how to cope in the world without using drugs. In our program, we ask for a minimum of 90 days, but many have stayed for a year or longer. It's not necessarily that they are afraid to leave; sometimes they are saving for an apartment or waiting for the next college semester to start. When they decide to stay beyond 90 days, they also start taking on a number of extra responsibilities within the organization that are geared toward helping the newest arrivals.

12-Step Program and Fellowship – This is the basis of most treatment curriculums and I believe the most important part of one's recovery. This is the step-by-step program in which we find true freedom from our addiction through self-sacrifice and service towards others. You may have visited a 12-step meeting and did not understand what was happening, but a meeting and the program are two different things. Just going to meetings doesn't change anything; we have to actually do the work and follow the directions we are given if we are to experience what has been offered. It's like going to college but never opening a book or doing homework. What happens in the classroom is just a small part of the educational process, and to get all you can out of it you have to follow the instructions and do the work.

WHY THIS TIME IS DANGEROUS

Human nature and survival instincts lead us to believe that we can somehow handle this phenomenon of addiction on our own. We don't believe that a well-planned aftercare program is necessary. We just want to get back to our old life, the one where we can manipulate our friends and family to get our way and return to the family home. We put on a good face, and our family is so excited with our newfound sobriety that they reinstate all of our privileges. Things return to the way they were before treatment. Even with all of the good intentions and self-will we can gather, left to our own devices, we find ourselves back in the very same situation, plagued with bad decisions. We've lost before we've even started.

We may have completed treatment or possibly a stay in the county jail, but everything starts to fall apart and we can't stay sober. We feel our lives slipping away like water running through our hands. A cloud of doubt and despair begins to settle on top of us. Growing increasingly hopeless, we start looking for the "off switch." Sadly—and far too often—this off switch can be taking our own lives. Addicted people are far more likely to commit suicide when they find themselves at a place where they do not believe they can live with drugs or live without them. We just feel trapped and cannot see any other way out, particularly in the beginning or after a relapse. It is more about stopping the noise and pain than leaving the earth.

To stay clean and sober on a permanent basis, we have to change everything about how we live, react, and treat people. Aftercare is specifically designed for this purpose because it teaches individuals how to be sober in a world full of setbacks, drugs, and alcohol. If we try to hide from everything, we are doomed before we even start.

The 12-step program, as outlined in the first 164 pages of the Basic Text of Alcoholics Anonymous, shows us how to live and treat others. A strong sober living program reinforces what we have learned and challenges us to expand our chances of staying sober by helping others. It is the lifeline of our recovery; we are not changing who we are, we are changing how we see the world and treat others. Your child will still be your child, but she will be a better, more independent, and more helpful version of your child.

But problems arise if she returns to her previous life and the family has not changed the way they treat her. Sometimes family members have a hard time adjusting to her spirit of independence and do not like the change. They have managed the details of their child's life for so long that they insist on continuing to do it. The rub comes when she asks the overstepping family member to stop. If there are codependency issues, this process can get uncomfortable quickly, and it may highlight the need for the family member to seek help for codependency issues. This may be as easy as going to Al-Anon and working the steps with a sponsor. As I explained previously, in extreme cases, the family member may need to seek treatment options.

My advice is that you let your child do as much as possible on her own. If she is 18 years or older, it is time for her to move out on her own and stand on her own two feet. Again, this is what a strong sober living program is for. Our organization will not accept applicants if the plan after 90 days is to just move home again. We are there to teach them how to be independent and pay their own way in life. Since we only house men and women 18 or older, they are all adults, whether the family thinks so or not. Allow them to return home and you could end up with a 40-year-old child in your home who cannot live on her own. We call this failure to launch, and it may well prevent your child from developing healthy relationships and the drive for a fulfilling career.

Consider that when individuals do not move forward they become emotionally handicapped. The resulting consequences are a lack of healthy relationships and meaningful careers and an inability to start a family of their own.

There are obviously times when your help is appropriate and even warranted, but always look at the situation and ask yourself questions such as these: Is it truly helpful, or are you allowing him to take the easy way out? Can he continue driving an old car or utilizing public transportation until he saves enough for a newer vehicle? Does he need an education, or is he hiding out in school, collecting one degree after another and never entering the workforce? Sometimes we are bus riders who work for minimum wage until we can improve our own circumstances. Fathers with great expectations for their children often have a problem with this. We must be allowed to do this. Struggle builds character, and if we are allowed to persevere we can accomplish much. Cheat us out of this growth and nothing will change.

Think about all of the hard choices and sacrifices you have made over the years to provide for yourself and your family. I remember when it was a choice between new shoes or food, or between buying a car and paying my rent. Many times I made the wrong choice and suffered the consequences, but these decisions have shaped who I am. This bears repeating: Adversity and struggle build character, just as suffering builds strength. Given the opportunity, your child can accomplish more than you might imagine, even if he has a criminal record resulting from his addiction.

There will be times when you disagree with the sponsor's directions or with boundaries they have set. It may be infuriating to hear your child make statements about leading a spiritual life after years of self-absorbed behaviors. It could feel as though she is growing away from the family and spending too much time with complete strangers. It may terrify you to learn that your child is actively seeking out others who are currently using.

Before launching into panic mode, talk to your child about these changes. There could be very virtuous reasons for each questionable behavior. Reasons such as working with others, surrounding herself with like-minded peers, or developing new and healthier hobbies.

I would be much more worried if your child appeared exhausted, isolated, or exaggeratedly emotional, but even these behaviors may be temporary and easily explained. It is when nothing appears to have changed that your child is at the greatest risk. Even though you desperately want things to go back to how they were before, you must remember that how things were before led to your child's problems. Given time and space to embrace her new life in recovery, she will become a better version of herself.

On the other hand, if your child is a minor and has returned home, you need to conduct random drug tests to keep a level of accountability and peace of mind that your child is clean. If you are uncertain about which drugs to test for or how accurate the drug test you are using is, go to a local lab. If your child continues the addictive behaviors, you need to find a higher level of care, which could be a children's home or even military school where there is a strict level of accountability and expectation. As hard as this may be, it could be what is best, especially if there are other children in your home.

The great thing about children's homes is that they typically do not cost much. However, they do not accept children who are 18, so you have a limited time for this option. Once your child is 18 you really cannot force him to go anywhere, which is why we always look for leverage. In this case, the leverage is the family home. You do not need leverage for a child under 18; you simply take him back to treatment or another available option.

You may feel as though you are abandoning your child, and he may even say as much, but you must keep your other children safe. Remember that your family is under attack and you must win. You are not pawning your child off on someone else; you are saving your family. There will be some who support your decision and some who condemn it. You have to decide what is more important to you: how you are viewed by others, or how thorough you are being in using every available tool to keep your child alive and the rest of your family safe.

If your child is 18 years of age or older and you have allowed him back into the home, you must remove him for the very same reasons. As hard as it may be to take him to a shelter or sober home, it is what is best for the entire family. He may refuse to go into the shelter or sober living facility; if so, he is deciding to be homeless on the spot. The only real power you have is to remove him from the family home and offer help. There are not many 18-year-olds who want to be homeless, so he will likely go where you have made arrangements, provided you do not crumble. If he is removed for relapse or non-compliance, you are to do as my father did and tell him you are sorry and want to hear how everything works out. Offer no money or hotel room. Doing this gives him the chance to work things out with the home or shelter. He will eventually learn how to comply with rules if you let him walk through his own self-imposed crisis.

It is a good idea to attend Al-Anon meetings and read the first 164 pages of the Basic Text of Alcoholics Anonymous. Work the steps yourself so that you can make decisions that are not based in fear and you will know what to expect. One of the benefits of working the steps is that we will intuitively know how to handle situations that used to baffle us. That alone is worth your time and a $10 book. You will also develop your own support group, comprised of other families who have walked in your shoes. Even if you are thinking that you are well adjusted and do not need help or support, take a hard look at your family and honestly evaluate the toll that addiction has taken on it. No family deals with this and comes out unscathed. If your spouse objects, saying he does not need anyone's help, approach the subject by suggesting that the two of you could help other families. If he refuses, go alone. Just go. It cannot hurt. Why would you be opposed to going? You have come so far and already have done so much to help your family. Why would you turn down further help that costs nothing but a few dollars and some time? Could it be that you do not want others to know your problems? Is that fear or arrogance? It always strikes me as a little odd when parents demand so much change from their child but are unwilling to experience any change themselves.

Much like the old saying, "A family that prays together stays together," I offer this: "A family that does recovery together heals together." Is that not what we all want?

To conclude this chapter I present the following key points:

- Allow your child to reap the consequences or benefits of her own decisions.
- Encourage her to continue in recovery.
- Do not freely give her money. If there is an appropriate need, such as first month's rent for sober living, PHP, IOP, or tuition, make the payment directly to the organization or educational institution. Never put cash in your child's hands. She has proven that she is unable to make wise decisions, and cash is a temptation

she does not need.
- Do not let your adult child back into the family home. Recovery means learning to stand on her own two feet.
- Do not give your child a job; let him learn how to find and hold his own job. If he is to join the family business one day, it should be after he has multiple years of sobriety, has demonstrated good choices, has learned from his mistakes, and has proven himself as a valuable employee, even if that means he is working in the fast food industry or has some other minimum wage job. He must learn the value of a job as well as the value of a dollar. If you allow this to happen, he can learn how to become a great employee, one worthy of taking over the family business. In the meantime, encourage him; offer books and tapes related to leadership skills that can fuel constructive conversations between the two of you concerning business practices and balance in life. Give him books and recordings from Zig Ziglar and encourage him to explore Ziglar's ideas about the healthy professional and the Wheel of Life.
- Stay out of the way of her recovery. If you cannot do this, you need to seek help for yourself. If you ignore this, you are increasing the odds that your child will return to her addictive behaviors. The best-case scenario here is that you start this painful and expensive process all over. The worst-case scenario is that you receive that call that no parent wants. So again, what is more important?

I know this has been difficult information to read and digest. I applaud you for reading to this point; you are a fighter. There are no easy shortcuts, no "three points and a poem" to make it all better. I am truly sorry if your family has been affected by addiction, and you are in my constant prayers. As I emerged from this pit of despair, I was challenged to make a difference and I have based my entire life on helping families just like yours. In this respect, we are all equals.

CHAPTER EIGHT

WHAT LIFE SHOULD LOOK LIKE IN LONG-TERM RECOVERY

The preceding chapters have laid out the road map to help move our addicted loved one to this point – long term recovery. By this phase of our recovery, we, the addicted, have become productive members of our community. People can count on us, and when we say we will do something it will actually happen. Others may set their watch by our punctuality and look to us for advice on troubling or complex situations. Families in need will seek us out for help, and there are people who are alive because they allowed us to take them through the steps and challenge them to help others in return. A host of friends that we consider as family has grown up around us. This and more become our reality when we make the spiritual principles we learned in the 12-step program a permanent part of our life.

Here is a list of the spiritual principles we strive to live by:

- Honesty
- Hope
- Faith
- Courage
- Integrity
- Willingness
- Humility
- Brotherly Love
- Justice
- Perseverance
- Spirituality
- Service

This list is easy enough to read through, but if we are to comprehend and submit to these principles, we find it best to work a 12-step program. If we do our best to live by these principles, we can recover.

The longer we practice these principles the easier our life becomes; so easy that we may ask ourselves why we waited so long to give in and become teachable. Even our bad decisions and selfish acts from the past become our greatest resources and strengths when working with others.

We strive to live by a code of patience, love, and tolerance. These core values must be present in all of our daily interactions in order to remain in a place of safety from our addiction. Much like being in remission, we must continue to take care of ourselves in order to stay ahead of our disease.

EMPLOYMENT

This is what life might look like as we begin to build, or rebuild, our careers. Most often we have burned so many bridges that we must start from scratch, which for many of us means finding that dreaded minimum wage job. We have to eat and pay our bills, so we need to enter the workplace with a good attitude, grateful for the opportunity to earn. It is possible that our future employer may look at our work history and ask why we deserve a chance. Our answer should be something like this: "I want to be completely honest. I am a recovered alcoholic/addict and I have been clean now for X amount of time. In order to beat my addiction once and for all, there are many things I must do, one of which is to stand on my own two feet and pay my own way in this world. To do that I need a job, and if you hire me I will be here every day." More often than not, we will be offered the job and can begin to live a *lean* life within a budget we can afford.

This may be our only earning potential at first, but we should make the best of it and become the best employee possible. Eventually, we will improve our situation through promotions or by moving on to a different company. In the meantime, we continue doing our very best and start to consider our future. Have we left our education unfinished, or have we decided on a new career that requires years of training? If further education is what we seek, we look for available higher education avenues, which may include community college, a state university, or an online learning institution. There are as many choices as there are funding programs. Some state universities offer a specialized track for men and women in recovery, which is paid for through federal grants. The pioneer school here is Texas Tech. The idea of offering this type of specialized program is growing across the country, making more programs available all the time. Many schools have very active collegiate recovery programs. These make it possible to easily connect with like-minded peers.

Once we decide what to do, we should let our employer know that we are taking courses to obtain a degree and promise to do our best to enroll in classes that do not disrupt our work schedule. Almost any employer will be willing to work around your schedule and encourage you along the way. If your employer says he cannot work around any changes, it is time to start looking for another job on your own time. As you look, you will need to explain that you will be attending school at the next available semester. Do not leave your job until you have secured a new one, and make sure you give ample notice; we are living under a new code, which insists that we are fair and honest. Lastly, you will need to consider how many hours you need for school, work, and a personal life. There must be some balance here; we do not have the same luxury as others who may burn the candle at both ends. If we do that, we are putting ourselves at grave risk.

We may find that we are in a position to move upward in the company to a great career. McDonalds often says they are responsible for making more millionaires than any other company. There are countless stories of people who started as fry cooks and then worked their way up into eventual ownership of one or more franchises. I am not suggesting that you forego an education to work at McDonalds; however, you may find that your current job combined with an education is a great career option.

We may find that we would be happiest working for ourselves and start our own companies. A man I know started pushing a mower when he got sober because he needed to make money and did not believe that anyone would hire him. He started mowing lawns, driving his truck from house to house. Within just a few years, he was making enough to hire a crew to mow yards for him, while he sought out more business. Within another year or two, he had a number of crews and he started designing high-end outdoor living spaces. Now he drives around in his new truck, checking on all of his crews and making more money than he ever thought possible.

The truth is that our inability to earn in the past was self-imposed, and our new lease on life has given us the ability to thrive. It does not matter where we came from, how much money our family has, or what our race is. If we live within the spiritual principles we were taught, we can accomplish almost anything. Another truth is that what we do for a living does not matter nearly as much as how happy and well balanced we are. Our career is merely to fund our lifestyle. If we love what we do, it will be all the better, but at the end of the day what matters is that we have a job, can pay our bills, and become self-sufficient.

Your child may find that his career comes easily but may not challenge or fulfill his desire to help others. Let's say your son is a mechanic. He has built a great reputation as being fair, honest, and a man of his word. He may not be passionate about his work, but he is good at what he does and has a great earning potential. Rather than risk becoming unsatisfied and deciding to do something different (which may not have the same earning potential), he could look for ways to incorporate his desire to help others into his business. There are a host of churches and nonprofit organizations that would benefit from an offer of free repairs. He may consider hiring someone who is just starting his new sober way of life. He can provide training and mentorship to give this person a career, provided the person is serious and willing to work for it. As he learns the most effective ways to advance the knowledge of his new hire, he may consider starting a program that employs a number of men and women who are just starting their new lives. This can increase his productivity and help him expand his business. Although he has the same career, he has added a whole new purpose. This line of thinking can be adapted to almost any business; it becomes a life-changing business that also happens to perform a service or produce goods.

If your child is an employee for someone else, he can integrate many of these ideas into his current job. He could be the employee whom management calls upon when someone within the company is struggling. This suddenly gives great purpose to an otherwise lackluster job and elevates him to an exceptional employee. Companies invest in great employees.

RELATIONSHIPS

Even our relationships now look different. Starting with our own family, we must realize that some level of distrust may exist for some time, but we do not argue the point nor do we demand to be treated differently. We have spent years earning the way we are treated and may need to spend years repairing our relationships.

Most of us eventually experience a far better relationship with our family than we ever thought possible. In some cases, we may never achieve this, but that must not stop us from continuing to be helpful and going on with our lives.

Romantic relationships should also look completely different. We have been taught how to check our motives and be honest. If we see someone whom we find attractive, we should ask ourselves, "Is this someone I would genuinely like to know? Am I interested in her welfare?" or, "Do I just want to do whatever I need to convince this person to have sex with me?" These are very simple questions, but we must be honest with ourselves before we can be good for anyone else. Our job is to enhance the lives of others and be completely transparent when it comes to our motives.

If we are acting one way in front of our friends, another in front of our family, another at church, and still another at work, we are still living a life of deception. We find that when we are the same person in all of our settings, we are truly doing our best to be honest. When we sincerely try to do the right thing, it comes easily to us, and the longer we try the easier it becomes. Given enough time, it becomes who we are, and others start characterizing us as consistent and trustworthy.

BALANCE

As we look for balance in our lives, we seek out hobbies and healthy activities that often involve a club or team. Look for something constructive that offers the benefits of recharging our batteries and keeping us grounded. Sometimes a hobby may turn into a career, giving us the ability to absolutely love what we do for a living. If this happens, we again strive for proper balance by finding another activity for a hobby or pastime.

We might find ourselves returning to a church where our new lives are embraced by others. We can join civic clubs or organizations that raise our level of productivity in our community. We may even be asked to hold a position of leadership where we can demonstrate the value of service.

DEALING WITH CHALLENGES

Fear and ego no longer have a death grip on us and when we feel them creeping back, we have our 12-step sponsor and our support system to help get us back on track. We know this is a lifetime process for us. Once in a while we see someone who was sober for many years throw it all away and lose everything. As shocking as it is, it is always the result of straying from our code and returning to isolation, fear, or ego. The markers of trouble were there long before the incident; they were just ignored. This is why after two decades, I still talk to my sponsor or some other mentor whenever I am troubled or about to make a huge life change. I need someone who really knows me to look at any situation and be completely honest about it. I am human, and therefore I make mistakes. I am able to sort most things out with prayerful consideration, but, at times, it is best to seek counsel. Even the President of the United States is surrounded by advisors who share their wise counsel.

What do we do about failure, when we feel we have done everything right? There is a host of factors we cannot control: markets crash, severe weather collapses buildings, items become obsolete, employees and/or customers take advantage of others, criminal activity victimizes businesses. The list goes on and on. These things may happen, and we may not have insurance; we may again be looking at financial ruin. It may be unfair and we may have been wronged, but we have a decision to make: Start over or lie down.

Thomas Edison was once asked about a recent failure and he replied, "I did not fail. I just learned another way that does not work."

I choose to start over. Early in sobriety I wasn't sure who would hire me, so I started a delivery company. Over the years, the success of my company allowed me to move to a bigger house in a better area and afforded me the opportunity to start my current organization. Just as we were really getting started with our new nonprofit, I was able to sell my delivery company to my financial advisor. He made a lump sum payment and was to pay off the balance over a number of years. The problem was he was not so good with operations. Within six months, he ran off all my drivers and bankrupted a viable company. He called to let me know that he was shutting down the company and would not be sending any more money.

After prayerful consideration and several discussions with my sponsor, I decided to take the man to court to honor our contract. We settled out of court for pennies on the dollar. This was supposed to be how I would get paid for the next several years while I put together my new organization. I could have panicked, closed shop, and returned to the workforce for a paycheck, but my wife and I decided to move forward. We decided to stretch our money as far as we could before closing down the organization, which was now saving lives. That was over a decade ago. I now have a staff and we are growing to meet the needs in our community. I am blessed to love my job and pay my bills. With every passing year, my organization becomes stronger and saves more lives. I am rich in ways I never imagined, ways that cannot be measured by money.

What about when tragedy strikes? What happens to the man or woman in recovery when someone close to them suddenly dies? If it is your child who endures this kind of sorrow, she will pass through all of the stages of grief and will need her support system more than ever. She simply cannot surround herself with too much help. There are amazing counselors and support groups to help her walk through this time with dignity and grace. This will keep her from reaching into her past for old coping mechanisms, which would only result in further tragedy. She will be able to walk through this; she has already overcome more than most will ever encounter.

Eventually, your child will be able to look at this in the same light as her recovery. Once she is able to receive help, she will find the most healing through helping others who are experiencing the same loss. There are no promises that her life will be perfect; there never were. There is only this: Her life will be enhanced by the amount of enrichment she gives others. In conclusion, what life looks like in long-term recovery is stable, happy, purposeful, and consistent.

CHAPTER NINE

A PERSONAL VIEW

I have shared bits and pieces of my own struggles and triumphs throughout the first eight chapters of this book. Here I will share a deeper view of what I have overcome and how, in recovery, I have walked through fire. I do this to show you that your addicted loved one can recover and find true happiness and sense of purpose.

I come from an upper middle class, loving family, with one older brother and one younger sister. My parents still live together in the very house they bought when we first came to Texas in the summer of 1976. I was to start the 5th grade.

Somewhere around the beginning of junior high, I started smoking pot and would drink alcohol when I could get my hands on it. Throughout high school, my friends and I always tried to buy beer, but we were not of drinking age; drugs were always easier to get. By the time we finished school, we had started to abuse a number of dangerous drugs. I was arrested for public intoxication on a number of occasions.

Many of my friends went to college, but I had no desire to do so. At 16, I was paid to play music for the very first time. At the front door of the Dallas nightclub, I was stopped and asked for my ID. Looking at the bouncer, I simply stated that I was there to play music. He quickly backed up and held the door open, saying, "I'm sorry man. Would you like a beer?" It was as if a new chapter of my life started at that very moment. I took the beer and headed to the stage to set up my equipment.

As night fell, people started entering the club, and before long we took the stage, playing as if our lives depended on everyone enjoying themselves. The more I heard people cheering, the more I felt as though I had finally arrived in life. Women were dancing and guys were pumping their fists to the beat of the music. I noticed one particular woman with dyed hair and tacky, short clothes, and I thought she was the coolest thing I ever saw. She made eye contact with me and continued dancing right up against the stage. At our first break, she came right up to me on stage, threw her arms around me, and kissed me, saying, "You know when this is over you are coming home with me." All I can remember thinking was, this was the greatest night of my life and why would anyone not want to do this for a living. I had stars in my eyes and spent the next 15 years chasing that dream.

I had always loved music and I started to study it in the 4th grade. Throughout my scholastic career, I competed in and won a number of University Interscholastic League (UIL) music competitions; I excelled the most at the sight-reading competitions. I was always in the top band at first chair until the night I played in a nightclub and lost all interest in the school band department. By this time, I was accomplished in all of the low brass, but I traded it in for the opportunity to strap an electric bass to myself and chase my dream of becoming a rock star. I was married to a woman named Rita at 21, but we divorced shortly afterwards as I did not make a good husband, and she deserved far better than I had to offer.

Professional musician, yes, rock star, no. My addiction started taking center stage, causing me to make frequent trips to the Dallas County Jail. This resulted in me missing some key opportunities, which eventually cost our band dearly. Ultimately, the band fired me. With different bands, I traveled across the country, chasing this dream of riches and fame. We always said that when we made it, we would be a band that showed up at local bars to spend time with fans. In reality, by the end all I wanted to do was get signed to a big contract. I wanted to make millions to buy a great big house with guard dogs and a big gate to keep everyone away from me. By now, I hated everyone but the members of my band, and even one of them I could do without.

Along the way, we lost our singer to a cocaine overdose at the age of 26. When this happened, all I could do was drink as much whisky and ingest as much cocaine as I could get; it was the only way I knew to blunt the pain of life. Somewhere in Dallas the wife and child of my recently deceased friend were trying to cope with this incredible tragedy, and all I could think about was how I had been cheated out of our big chance at fame. He was not the first friend to die, nor was he the last; the truth is that people were dropping all around me from drug overdoses and booze-fueled accidents.

Soon afterwards, I was arrested again for my public display of drunkenness, and I spent a number of months

in jail. Once I was released, I had to find a new singer to
get back on the road. We started earning again, and I
was living the life I so desperately wanted—until my
next trip to jail. Over and over I put it all back together,
living by a separate set of rules and in a different
lifestyle from ordinary people. We always started to
play between 10 and 11 p.m. and played until 2 a.m.,
which is when the real party would start. The women I
became involved with lived by the same rules and
lifestyle as I did.

We became so jaded that even our business plan was
corrupt. We would go out in the late afternoon to the
gentlemen's club and start throwing around money and
talking to the dancers. We told them we were playing
later that night and that there would be a lot of cocaine
and alcohol. Daytime dancers finish their shift at 7 p.m.
with a pile of cash and are ready to party all night.
When they showed up at the clubs, it drove the guys
crazy and they would then spend more money at the bar.
They saw advertisements for our next show, and they
would tell their friends, "These guys rock the house and
they have the most amazing women at their shows! We
have got to go see them!"

This worked in any city at any bar, and club owners
loved the turnout. Toward the end, I knew that I could
not stay sober all day and be able to perform at 11 p.m. I
would get up and get drunk so I could go back to sleep
and set my alarm for 9 p.m. This way I could take the
stage with beer in hand and make it through the next four
hours without being too drunk to play. Those three to
four hours on the stage became the only thing in life that
mattered; everything else was just time I spent waiting
before I could again feel normal and have some sense of
enjoyment in life. Without music, I might have ended it

all, as my prayers were, "God, if you are real please just kill me tonight because I don't think I can take this anymore."

Jail was becoming a bigger hindrance in my career. I had a judge who knew I was a drug addict and decided to take certain actions to keep me alive. I thought he hated me, but the truth was he knew that if he sent me to prison, I would soon be out and he would have no control over my actions. He also knew I would re-offend or end up dead on the streets of Dallas, so he would not let me off the probation hook. That meant he regularly had me placed in jail with a probation hold so I could not bond out.

My dad told me one day that if I kept getting arrested I would never be able to get a good job. I replied, "Dad, a rock star who has never been to jail is called a poser. This is what's making my résumé."

Another consequence of my lifestyle was getting robbed at gunpoint on four different occasions. You would think I would learn to stay out of such circumstances, but I had a real knack for always being in the wrong place at the wrong time.

One day I sat down and attempted to count just how many times I had been arrested and just how much time I had spent sitting in the Dallas County jail system. With all of the public intoxications, failures to appear, various probation violations (mostly non-payment and no-show), two DWIs, and a possession of a controlled substance, I believe the number of arrests equals 42. From the age of 17 to 30 I spent almost all 13 years on probation, and I spent a total of 2½ years sitting in the Dallas County Jail. All of this just because I wanted to be drunk or high.

As soon as any band I was in started making money and playing for large crowds on a consistent basis, I would do something stupid and inevitably catch the attention of the police. Once they ran my numbers it was off to jail every single time. Jail cost me every lease I signed, every truck I bought, every job, and eventually every band. It's hard enough to make it in the entertainment industry, but when you cost your bandmates a number of really good chances because you have been arrested, they get pretty mad and get rid of you. At some point, talent and hard work aren't enough to excuse the ruined opportunities you have cost the band.

It was a huge blow to my ego when I was fired and they went on without me. By this time, my addiction was so out of control that the only reason I wanted to live was for the few hours at night that I was on stage. Everything else was painful. I just wanted to write and play my music, but jail kept getting in the way.

TRYING FOR SOBRIETY

I would make good money working in a bar or an automotive shop, but I felt as though I was a failure. I resented the judge and I resented the county for ruining my life. I knew if I continued to drink and use drugs that I would continue to go to jail, and that had to stop. For a few weeks I basically sat on my hands and white-knuckled it, surrounding myself with people in a 12-step program. Before I had completed 30 days I was pulled over for looking shady, and because I owed money and had missed a few appointments, I was taken back to jail. This time as I sat in the holding tank, a prosecutor entered and said, "You just are not any good at this whole idea of probation." He dropped my overly stuffed file on the table with a thud and looked at me. "We are done with you and we are just going to let you do five years flat."

I agreed and told the man that five years might just be what I needed to get a handle on things. When pushed and asked why I had suddenly become willing to just lie down and accept five years in jail, I replied, "You probably won't believe me, but I have been sober for 30 days and I have no idea what I am doing. When you say five years, I hear a five-year head start to put my life together. I have absolutely no idea how I am going to make it, so just file whatever you have to file and send me on my way."

He then told me that all they had ever wanted to hear was my desire to get clean and remain sober. He explained that they would give me one more chance. In my mind I thought this must mean more years of probation, but what they wanted to do was place me under house arrest for six months and give me the opportunity to get well. If I could do this for six months, I would be released from probation; if I could not, I would do five years flat. Either way, my probation career was finally coming to an end. I accepted their offer.

I was able to remain sober for that six months, and I have been sober ever since. This was in 1995 and I have not been charged with anything new or returned to Dallas County Jail since.

After I was fired that last time, the band went on to enjoy televised specials and open for acts like Mötley Crüe. Opportunities like that get you national attention, large

tours, and larger pay, but I never got to enjoy any of it.
I thought if I could get sober I might be able to take the
stage again, but I could not seem to get a band together.
It was as though it had been taken off the table for good.
I had earned two reputations: one as a great showman,
and the other as the person who will get thrown in jail at
a pivotal moment. The only musicians I could find who
were willing to work with me either lacked any real
talent or could not stay sober themselves.

This is the one activity I was not willing to let go of, but
it was also the thing that might have killed me. I so
desperately wanted to return, but I now believe that God
was doing something for me that I was unable to do for
myself.

About two years into my recovery, I married a beautiful,
tall, blonde woman named Kathy. She had a corporate
job and a nice apartment, so it was amazing to me that
she wanted to have anything to do with me. I had started
a delivery company earlier and earned a decent living, so
I was not a deadbeat. I just thought I was a failed
musician trying to make do and was surprised that she
was interested in me.

The night came when I told her that while I did not want
to drink or get high, I simply could not stomach one
more 12-step meeting. If I heard one more grown man
talk about his ex-wife or bad job, I might reach across
the table and smack him. She agreed and said she
wanted to introduce me to someone and go to one more
meeting. If I felt the same way afterwards, we would
never return.

That night I met the man who became my sponsor and
still is today. He pointed out that I was miserable

because I had never actually done the step work, and just went to meetings where I listened to other people who had not done the work. He explained how I could have a great life if I would just be willing to do some work related to how I lived. I agreed and we immediately started to do the work. A short time later, I felt relief as I never had before; I was actually looking forward to the next day.

I got well, but I started to watch my wife struggle with a deep depression and bipolar disorder. We loved each other, but another human cannot fix the hole inside one's soul. She went from one doctor to another, experiencing manic episodes followed by days of total silence. When we were dating, sometimes she would tell me that she had had a long week and just wanted to stay in over the weekend. At the time, it seemed like a reasonable request. I would later learn that she was actually laying out all of her meds, trying to decide whether she wanted to commit suicide or not. I had no idea about her state of mind, nor could I imagine that just a few years after we were married she would commit suicide.

Our relationship was tumultuous, but one day, with a big smile, she told me that she was pregnant. It seemed as though all was well for the moment, but then she had a miscarriage and we both fell apart. I isolated myself, and she sought peace in the many prescription drugs she had acquired from her doctors. At the time, I assumed that all prescription drugs were good for you if the doctor prescribed them, but as many of us have learned, that is not always the case. A short time later she took her own life.

Even though this relationship was difficult, I loved her deeply, and when she was gone I became very distant and angry. I was angry with almost everyone, including and especially God. Why would He let me experience all of this just to take it all away? Why couldn't I have just turned left instead of right and never met Kathy? Why had I been given the promise of a family just to lose everything? I became aggravated every time someone stood around me mumbling in an attempt to find words to make me feel better, and I absolutely hated it when people said that time heals everything. I mostly found people irritating, so during my time off I isolated myself in a small rental house where I often just sat and cried.

I was mad at God, but I did not want to drink, so I continued to visit an East Texas treatment center where I could talk to their clients. One night there was a fresh group of men who had just been released from Substance Abuse Felony Punishment, a Texas prison treatment system. Much like me, these men had been in and out of jail their entire adult lives, and they had been conditioned to believe that this was how their lives would be until the day they died. No one had ever told them they could break the cycle and live free lives. I told them about my past and how I was forever done with drugs and jail; I let them know they could do the same and create the life they once dreamed of. By the end of the hour, there was barely a dry eye in this room full of tough men who believed they were not worthy of happiness and freedom. I had not mentioned Kathy, but when I returned to my truck I broke down and sobbed, again asking God why He would let this happen.

Did I not do my best to help His children?

Later that night, I returned home to one of our famous severe Texas thunderstorms. I stood in my backyard looking up to the sky screaming "F*** you!" Shooting my middle finger from each hand upwards, I just repeated myself and fell to my knees, weeping uncontrollably for what felt like hours. The winds raged and the rain fell all night while thunder and lightning filled the sky. I do not remember getting up out of the mud; I just remember waking up in my house.

Later that day, a woman from my work showed up at my house with a bucket of fried chicken and a desire to comfort me. A few days later, another woman I know did the same thing. It seemed as though all I did for the next several months was go to work, speak at the treatment center, and stay in all weekend just to be surprised by who would show up and with what intentions. I started to wonder if this was how my life was going to look, just aimlessly wandering about, going from the arms of one woman to the next. I asked for none of it, but it started feeling more and more like my past.

One person I kept in touch with was my sponsor. As I felt I was starting to lose my grip on things, I started attending 12-step meetings again in conjunction with my visits to the treatment center. Before long, I was attending a meeting or treatment center every weeknight, and I often returned home to find a note on my door saying, "I was here but you were not," complete with a lipstick kiss impression.

I started to hear about others who, like Kathy, had taken their lives. Often this happened just after they left jail or treatment. It seemed like an epidemic, so I started taking a role in helping find placement for those who were leaving the East Texas treatment center where I volunteered. I quickly learned that without resources, most of these men and women had nowhere to go but the very environments that had led to their troubles in the first place. The more involved I got, the more alarming the numbers seemed.

Many would recommit crimes just to go back to a world of incarceration, which was sometimes the only life that made sense. Others died at their own hands because they couldn't bear life anymore. Feeling good and inspired while in a protective environment was one thing, but going out into the world was completely different. I believe this is how many people become institutionalized.

Thoughts started pouring into my head that something had to be done, but how could I, a complete mess, do anything about it? I wasn't even leading a respectable life. I just wanted to do something to help keep people out of the ground.

Eventually I met Leslie, who would become my wife. I did not think that I really had anything to offer her, but something inside of me knew that this would not be another one-night stand or occasional weekend visit at my home. She had three children, which would usually have caused me to run, but I knew that this would either be everything or it would be nothing.

After we married, I decided to resurrect my delivery company. I had let it lie dormant for a time while I worked at the local Ford dealership replacing automatic transmissions. With the delivery company online again, we moved from East Texas to the Dallas–Fort Worth area, ending up in Denton County. This put me much closer to the airport where most of my freight originated or terminated, and the savings in fuel by living 65 miles closer to the airport made buying a new house an easy choice.

A short time later, we were encouraged to join our neighbors at church, which I had avoided since the passing of Kathy. I tried to talk my way out of it, but since these particular neighbors would not let up, we went. There I saw a minister who dressed casually and spoke my language. He often spoke of addiction and mental health. He said that people who work the steps and live by spiritual principles find true happiness and purpose in life, while others, who just show up at church and do nothing to change their lives, are often lost.

One Sunday he talked about how each of us has a specific purpose, and that many of us had no idea yet what that was. He went on to say that some of us know exactly what our purpose is, but for one reason or another could not perform it. He even said that some of us had thought it through and made plans but possibly could not afford to make the change. He then stated that he did not know if this was the right time or not, but he felt as though we should pull out our old plans and take a look at them in a new light. Possibly we would realize that now was the time to move towards our true purpose.

I had told Leslie that I wanted to provide a place for men and women to live while learning how to apply new principles to their new lives. I calculated that I needed $365,000, which I did not have, so I never moved past my written plans. On this day, we looked at each other as though the minister was speaking directly to us and decided to start looking at the possibility of moving forward. Within months, I found some property and decided to sign a lease with just the $4,500 that I had raised by calling friends and telling them of my plans.

Everything came together and our new organization was born.

Leslie had struggled a bit with my desire to jump in head first, as well as coping with her own friends and family who suffer from addiction, so she also worked through the same steps that had saved my life. This has made her an expert in working with the families of those we house in our facilities.

Over the next decade, we would grow beyond belief and find the life we had dreamed of. I now understand that everything I had endured prepared me for what I do today.

I no longer get angry when someone says that time heals all, but I do let them know they are mistaken. Time helps the pain become more manageable, but it never completely goes away. In fact, as I have been writing this chapter, I have broken down and cried a number of times. Sometimes a movie or song will cause the raw emotions to come flooding back in as though Kathy had died yesterday, or the miscarriage of my unborn child was this morning. I do not revel in morbid reflection, but sometimes it just comes in waves, almost like I am supposed to remember how it felt.

When someone dies, there is so much blame. There is an entire family that feels if I had been a better man Kathy would still be alive. Others are just confused about how to help. I will tell you the very best thing you can do for someone experiencing a loss is to just be there for them. You don't need to say anything; your presence says it all. I appreciate my friends who just wanted to spend time with me, and most of all I appreciate the man who held me accountable and helped guide me through this terrible time.

I had once thought that nothing good could come from my marriage to Kathy, but I was wrong. Everything about my life today has been affected by this relationship. If not for her, I would have never found the man who became my sponsor and took me through the work. I would have never paid attention to what happened after the men and women I talked to left treatment or jail. I would not have ever considered housing them so that they might have a fighting chance at life in a world where they had always failed. I do not believe I would still be alive today.

The most significant gift from my relationship with Kathy was Leslie. Had I never moved to East Texas to escape the noise and pain I saw everywhere in Dallas, I would have never met her. Without Leslie and her expertise in business and family matters, the organization I started would have never grown to the size it is today. Everything I have today—and everything I am allowed to do—is a direct result of these two women.

My path has been filled with many twists and turns. There are so many instances where I could have been killed or locked up forever. It is a seemingly vulnerable path that could have changed at any moment if I had just made a different choice. When I think about it, I wonder what would have happened if I had just changed one thing. Would I not have the life I enjoy today? Would I have never met Kathy or Leslie and have no happiness or sense of purpose? It almost frightens me to think that I could have derailed the delicate string of events and never realized my true potential. Would I care about anyone other than myself? Could I have returned to the stage and made good on my dreams? Would I have

210 · A VIEW

taken my own life behind the gates of a large house?

But the fact is that this delicate timeline is actually not so delicate. I do not question God's reasons or timeline anymore; I am exactly where I am supposed to be, doing exactly what I am supposed to be doing. There are many things I do not understand, or necessarily like, but I accept them. Struggle and adversity make for strength and resolve. What I do know is I have been given the ability to help others and I have based my life today on just that.

Today I have raised three children as my own and have a great relationship with my entire family. I have become a leader in my community. I have been able to effect change in the judicial community to better help those men and women who want the help and are willing to do whatever it takes to get well. Law enforcement is my strong friend and ally and is responsible for sending many men and women to us for help. I serve on the treatment team for our drug court, and an associate does the same on our mental health court. I have built a team of men and women, most of whom have come through our program, who now dedicate their time to helping others. We have a number of projects with our city and county to continue and enlarge our service.

This is what a nobody drug addict from Dallas with multiple arrests and years of jail can do if he just puts his mind to it. I have been clean and sober since March 20, 1995, and countless people are alive today because I decided to help.

This is no greater than what your child could do. As I said early in this book, there are no guarantees that you will not receive that call you fear the most, but you are the greatest resource and influence to help your child make better decisions. If you have already suffered a loss, I know exactly what you have been going through. I know that you can find a meaningful purpose in life and help others.

I have sat with many families throughout the years who have lost a loved one to this hideous disease. Sometimes a wave comes over me and I break down and cry. I do not always know why I am crying, but I believe it is often for others. Leslie has found me like this on more than one occasion. I assure her that it is not a reflection on our relationship. She just comforts and loves me.

I am so grateful for Leslie. When we added a property to help women, it was Leslie who said we should name the property "Kathy's House" to honor her memory.

APPENDICES

APPENDIX I

American Society of Addictive Medicine

2016 Facts and Figures

- Drug overdose is the leading cause of accidental death in the U.S., with 47,055 lethal drug overdoses in 2014. Opioid addiction is driving this epidemic, with 18,893 overdose deaths related to prescription pain relievers, and 10,574 overdose deaths related to heroin in 2014.

- From 1999 to 2008, overdose death rates, sales, and substance use disorder treatment admissions related to prescription pain relievers increased in parallel. The overdose death rate in 2008 was nearly four times the 1999 rate; sales of prescription pain relievers in 2010 were four times those in 1999; and the substance use

disorder treatment admission rate in 2009 was six
times the 1999 rate.

- In 2012, 259 million prescriptions were written
  for opioids, which is more than enough to give
  every American adult their own bottle of pills.

- Four in five new heroin users started out
  misusing prescription painkillers.

- Ninety-four percent of respondents in a 2014
  survey of people in treatment for opioid addiction
  said they chose to use heroin because prescription
  opioids were "far more expensive and harder to
  obtain."

Impact on Special Populations

Adolescents (12 to 17 years old)

- In 2014, 467,000 adolescents were current
  nonmedical users of pain relievers, with 168,000
  having an addiction to prescription pain relievers.

- In 2014, an estimated 28,000 adolescents had
  used heroin in the past year, and an estimated
  16,000 were current heroin users. Additionally,
  an estimated 18,000 adolescents had a heroin use
  disorder in 2014.

- People often share their unused pain relievers, unaware of the dangers of non-medical opioid use. Most adolescents who misuse prescription pain relievers are given them for free by a friend or relative.

- The prescribing rates for prescription opioids among adolescents and young adults nearly doubled from 1994 to 2007.

Women

- Women are more likely to have chronic pain, be prescribed prescription pain relievers, be given higher doses, and use them for longer time periods than men. Women may become dependent on prescription pain relievers more quickly than men.

- Between 1999 and 2010 prescription pain reliever overdoses led to the deaths of 48,000 women.

- Prescription pain reliever overdose deaths among women increased more than 400% from 1999 to 2010, compared to 237% among men.

- Heroin overdose deaths among women have tripled in the last few years. From 2010 through 2013, female heroin overdoses increased from 0.4 to 1.2 per 100,000.

It is important to point out that many of the drugs sold on the street are the same drugs that many people have prescriptions for.

APPENDIX II

Examples of Drugs (AKA Controlled Substances) and Their Corresponding Penalty Group

1	Cocaine, heroin, methamphetamine, GHB, ketamine, oxycodone, and hydrocodone.
1A	LSD
2	Ecstasy (MMDA/Molly), PCP, mescaline (resinous extractives of Cannabis that aren't marijuana, e.g., hashish, concentrated marijuana oil, wax)
3	Valium, Xanax, and Ritalin.
4	Compounds containing Dionine, Motofen, Buprenorphine, or Pryovalerone

Penalties for Drug Possession in Texas

Whether you are charged with felony possession or misdemeanor possession depends on the penalty group and the weight or amount of the drug.

Penalty Group 1

WEIGHT	CLASS	PENALTY
Less than 1 gram	State jail felony	180 days to 2 years in a state jail and/or a fine of not more than $10,000
1 gram or more, but less than 4 grams	Third-degree felony	2 to 10 years in a state prison and/or a fine of not more than $10,000
4 grams or more, but less than 200 grams	Second-degree felony	2 to 20 years in a state prison and/or a fine of not more than $10,000
200 grams or more, but less than 400 grams	First-degree felony	5 to 99 years in a state prison and/or a fine of not more than $10,000
400 grams or more	Enhanced first-degree felony	10 to 99 years and a fine of not more than $100,000

Penalty Group 1A

AMT	CLASS	PENALTY
Fewer than 20 units	State jail felony	180 days to 2 years in a state jail and/or a fine of not more than $10,000
20 or more units, but less than 80 units	Third-degree felony	2 to 10 years in a state prison and/or a fine of not more than $10,000
80 units or more, but less than 4,000 units	Second-degree felony	2 to 20 years in a state prison and/or a fine of not more than $10,000
4,000 units or more, but less than 8,000 units	First-degree felony	5 to 99 years in a state prison and/or a fine of not more than $10,000
8,000 units or more	Enhanced first-degree felony	15 to 99 years in a state prison and a fine of not more than $250,000

Penalty Group 2

WEIGHT	CLASS	PENALTY
Less than 1 gram	State jail felony	180 days to 2 years in a state jail and/or a fine of not more than $10,000
More than 1 gram, but less than 4 grams	Third-degree felony	2 to 10 years in a state prison and/or a fine of not more than $10,000
More than 4 grams, but less than 400 grams	Second-degree felony	2 to 20 years in a state prison and/or a fine of not more than $10,000
400 grams or more	Enhanced first-degree felony	5 to 99 years in a state prison and/or a fine of not more than $50,000

Penalty Groups 3 and 4

WEIGHT	CLASS	PENALTY
Less than 28 grams	Class A misdemeanor	Not more than 1 year in a county jail and/or a fine of not more than $4,000
28 grams or more, but less than 200 grams	Third-degree felony	2 to 10 years in a state prison and/or a fine of not more than $10,000
200 grams or more, but less than 400 grams	Second-degree felony	2 to 20 years in a state prison and/or a fine of not more than $10,000
400 grams or more	Enhanced first-degree felony	5 to 99 years in a state prison and/or a fine of not more than $50,000

APPENDIX III

Outline for the First 164 Pages of the

Basic Text of Alcoholics Anonymous

This is the ONLY book that gives us the clear-cut directions for taking the 12 steps.

The four different forwards include important information, such as why this book was published as well as certain historical A.A. facts. On page XIII, in the very first sentence, it states, "Men & Women who have *recovered,*" not who are in recovery or on the beam. (I recommend that you keep a dictionary close at hand for reference when studying this text.) Page XX gives us a historical breakdown of the percentage of people who stayed sober when they followed the directions of this text as of 1955. (These numbers reflect the information that was current 16 years after the first printing.)

The Doctor's Opinion – Pgs. XXIII–XXX These are two separate letters from Dr. Silkworth in which he describes the allergic reaction of alcohol on an alcoholic's mind and body. Since 1934 this has all been proven as medical fact.

Chapter 1 "Bill's Story" Pgs. 1–16 This is our co-founder's personal story. Look for the similarities rather than the differences between his story and your own, particularly on pages 5–8 where he describes the hellish nightmares of alcoholism and addiction.

Chapter 2 "There is a Solution" Pgs. 17–29 As the title suggests, this chapter addresses the fact that no matter how bad off we are, there is a solution to our problems. There are descriptive profiles of the different types of drinkers. This chapter describes what is required and what will come as we start our journey.

Chapter 3 "More About Alcoholism" Pgs. 30–43 This chapter gives us more examples of out of control alcoholics and gives us the ability to diagnose ourselves as alcoholics. Self-diagnosis is covered in the last paragraph on page 31 and the top of page 32.

Chapter 4 "We Agnostics" Pgs. 44–57 This chapter starts off with yet another method to diagnose ourselves in the very first paragraph. Most of the rest of the chapter deals with the ability to have faith and gives us specific guidelines for developing faith. The last four lines of page 46 contain these guidelines. They are very clear. Note that the idea of God or Higher Power is generalized to avoid prejudices and connections to specific religious beliefs. This is only a beginning; as one completes the work, the ideas of faith and God will become very clear.

Chapter 5 "How it Works" Pgs. 58–71 Up to this point in the book we have learned what an alcoholic and an addict are, if we are one, there is hope, what would be required of us if we were to recover, where we stood on faith, and if this program was indeed for us. This chapter lays out the program for us (pgs. 59–60) and follows it with the Third Step prayer on page 63. Next the text presents directions for three separate fourth Step inventories: a resentment inventory on pages 64–67, a fears inventory on page 68, and a sex conduct inventory on pages 68–69.

Chapter 6 "Into Action" Pgs. 72–88 Just as the title indicates, we go into immediate action. This chapter takes us through Steps 5 through 11 in a timely manner. Notice that throughout this chapter we are always directed to immediately move on and not slow down or take time off for personal understanding and reflection.

- **Step 5 Pgs. 72–75**
- **Steps 6, 7, and 8 Pg. 76**
- **Steps 8 and 9 Pgs. 76–84**
- **Step 10 Pgs. 84–85**
- **Step 11 Pgs. 85–88**

Chapter 7 "Working With Others" Pgs. 89–103 This entire chapter is devoted to taking the Twelfth Step. It shows us exactly how to sponsor someone by taking him or her through the steps. Although this text was written in 1936, this chapter covers every possible scenario you can and will encounter if you choose to carry this message. If you are a real alcoholic and/or addict and choose NOT to carry this message, you WILL drink or use again; there are no shortcuts.

Chapter 8 "To Wives" Pgs. 104–121 This chapter explains to our wives (spouse/partner) what has happened to us and what will become of us. An informed spouse can aid the healing process, help others, and understand what is happening and why. This chapter is the basis for Al-Anon.

Chapter 9 "The Family Afterward" Pgs. 122–135 Much like "To Wives," this chapter is for our families and is designed to support their understanding of what we are going through and if we are serious about recovery or not. It empowers them to reach out and help other families whether their family member recovers or not. This will also direct us in our dealings with a protégé's family. We don't just take an individual; we take on the whole family, even if our man/woman decides not to pursue the program but the family does.

Important Note: Look at the last three lines on page 135. Yes, you have probably seen them in print on the walls at a meeting, but you must understand that these are for our family to help them deal with us. THEY ARE NOT SLOGANS FOR US!

Chapter 10 "To Employers" Pgs. 136–150 This chapter provides directions for bringing A.A. into the workplace. It will give our employers the ability to understand employees who want and require help as well as spotting alcoholics who are not serious about the help and when to let them go. Correct knowledge of the program can only bring good into the workplace.

Chapter 11 "A Vision for You" Pgs. 151–164 In 1936 when this text was first printed, most cities had no A.A. This chapter gives the directions for bringing A.A. to new places and starting new groups. Anyone who is serious about finding and obtaining our solution can use this text to take the steps and carry the message to countless individuals. One person can change the lives of thousands; this is what we MUST do to survive.

APPENDIX IV

Resources

12 Step Substance Abuse Programs

Alcoholics Anonymous – (AA) www.aa.org

Drug Addicts Anonymous-(DAA) www.daausa.org

Narcotics Anonymous – (NA) www.na.org

Cocaine Anonymous – (CA) www.ca.org

Heroin Anonymous – (HA) www.heroin-anonymous.org

Crystal Meth Anonymous–(CMA) www.crystalmeth.org

Marijuana Anonymous-(MA) www.marijuana-anonymouse.org

Process Addictions

Overeaters Anonymous-(OA) www.oa.org

Gamblers Anonymous-(GA) www.gamblersanonymous.org

Sexaholics Anonymous-(SA) www.sa.org

For The Family

Al-Anon/Alateen www.al-anon.alateen.org

Nar-Anon www.nar-anon.org

Co-Anon (Cocaine Anonymous) www.co-anon.org

Scott Wisenbaker

Solutions of North Texas

PO Box 448 Denton, TX 76202

www.sontx.org

(940) 898-6202

Printed in Great Britain
by Amazon

20461972R00132